Designing
Middle and High School
Instruction
and
Assessment

Designing
Middle and High School
Instruction
and
Assessment

Using
the
Cognitive
Domain

John L. Badgett

Edwin P. Christmann

CORWIN
A SAGE Company

Copyright © 2009 by Corwin

For information:

 Corwin
A SAGE Company
2455 Teller Road
Thousand Oaks, California 91320
(800) 233-9936
Fax: (800) 417-2466
www.corwinpress.com

SAGE India Pvt. Ltd.
B 1/I 1 Mohan Cooperative
    Industrial Area
Mathura Road, New Delhi 110 044
India

SAGE Ltd.
1 Oliver's Yard
55 City Road
London EC1Y 1SP
United Kingdom

SAGE Asia-Pacific Pte. Ltd.
33 Pekin Street #02-01
Far East Square
Singapore 048763

Printed in the United States of America.

Library of Congress Cataloging-in-Publication Data

Badgett, John L.
Designing middle and high school instruction and assessment: Using the cognitive domain/John L. Badgett, Edwin P. Christmann.
    p. cm.
Includes bibliographical references and index.
    ISBN 978-1-4129-7117-1 (cloth) — ISBN 978-1-4129-7118-8 (pbk.)   1.   Middle school education—Curricula—United States.   2.   Education, Secondary—Curricula—United States.   3.   Lesson planning—United States.   4.   Educational tests and measurements—United States—Design and construction.   5.   Academic achievement—United States—Testing. I.   Christmann, Edwin P., 1966- II. Title.

LB1628.5.B33 2009
373.13'028—dc22   2008053031

This book is printed on acid-free paper.

09   10   11   12   13   10   9   8   7   6   5   4   3   2   1

Acquisitions Editor:	Dan Alpert
Associate Editor:	Megan Bedell
Production Editor:	Libby Larson
Copy Editor:	Marilyn Power Scott
Typesetter:	C&M Digitals (P) Ltd.
Proofreader:	Caryne Brown
Indexer:	Terri Corry
Cover Designer:	Karine Hovsepian

Contents

Acknowledgments

Emotional support is prerequisite to the success of virtually any major undertaking. Fortunately, our wives, Becky and Roxanne, and our children, Kathi, Les, Jennifer, Jesse, Lauren, Forrest, and Alexandra, were there for us from the outset to the completion of the book, as was Big Ed.

An inseparable fusion of strong emotional support and extraordinary professional assistance exceeds the dreams of most authors. Luckily, that is precisely what we had in John Hoyle, longtime mentor, colleague, and cherished friend; Dan Alpert, our editor consummate; Lisa Stiehler and Jessica Schroeffel, our irreplaceable research associates; Cindy Pulkowski, our nomenclator; Marilyn Scott, our patient and empathic copy editor; and Libby Larson, our insightful and meticulous project editor. Thanks, friends.

Also, we wish to express our appreciation to the following reviewers for their helpful suggestions.

Lyman Goding, Retired Principal
Sandwich, MA

John Hoyle, Professor of Educational Administration and Human
    Resource Development
Texas A&M University, College Station, TX

Nancy Kellogg, Professional Development Coordinator
Center for Learning and Teaching in the West
Boulder, CO

About the Authors

John L. Badgett received a PhD in Curriculum and Instruction from Texas A&M University. He is a professor at Slippery Rock University, where he received an Outstanding Teacher Award in 2007. He teaches both graduate and undergraduate courses in measurement and assessment to all education majors, as well as graduate courses in quantitative and qualitative research methods. He has taught social studies and English–language arts at both the elementary and the secondary levels. With Dr. Christmann, he has conducted and published many research studies relevant to this book. Moreover, they are the authors of the recently published *Interpreting Assessment Data: Statistical Techniques You Can Use.*

Edwin P. Christmann, professor and chair of the secondary education department and previous graduate coordinator of Slippery Rock University's mathematics and science teaching program, earned his PhD at Old Dominion University. He serves as a contributing editor to the National Science Teachers Association's middle schools journal, *Science Scope,* serves on the editorial review boards of several other journals, and has authored the book *Technology-Based Inquiry for Middle School* and coauthored *Interpreting Assessment Data: Statistical Techniques You Can Use.* He currently teaches graduate-level courses in measurement and assessments, science education, and statistics, which are built on the foundation of his math and science experiences in the public schools.

Introduction

The instruction and assessment practices of the nation's schools have come under criticism because of their perceived focus on the rote memorization of factual information. We see the acquisition of facts not as an end in itself, however, but as a foundation upon which higher-order teaching and testing can be built. Hence, we use the cognitive hierarchy of Bloom's Taxonomy (Bloom, Engelhart, Furst, Hill, & Krathwohl, 1956) to demonstrate how you can guide your students through increasingly complex thinking skills and assess proficiency with multiple forms of assessment at each level. It is important to remember that there is no single form of assessment that is applicable to all performances at each hierarchical level.

The underlying assumption of this book is that instruction for middle and high school students should proceed in an orderly fashion, from the general to the specific and from the simple to the complex. Just as our content examples serve as models for this progression within the Taxonomy for math, science, social studies, and English–language arts, they also serve as examples for this type of teaching in specialty areas, such as art, music, physical education, modern languages, and technology. You can simply adapt the model to the specialty area.

We advocate a four-step model of planning that entails a logical progression from (1) content area standards to (2) modified standards to (3) unit plan objectives to (4) daily instructional objectives in an understandable sequence of increasing specificity. Moreover, our view of teaching and assessment within each of the content areas is a progression from the Knowledge to the Evaluation levels of Bloom's Taxonomy (Bloom et al., 1956). This sequence is embedded in the interrelationship between instruction and assessment within the curriculum.

While the curriculum is largely driven by state and national standards, many teachers are confounded or even intimidated by the vagueness and lack of detail in the language of the standards. We hope that the easy-to-follow, general-to-specific model proposed in Chapter 1,

Deconstructing the Standards, helps to alleviate these concerns. This chapter shows you how to create clear and precise instructional objectives for various content areas as prescribed by national and state standards. You learn to deconstruct the broad-sweeping goals of the standards and transform them into unit plan objectives (more specific) and daily instructional objectives (most specific). We guide you through modifying the original standards and then designing unit plans around them, which ultimately serve as the basis for your daily instructional objectives. The examples are built around national content area standards, and you can easily adapt the model for use with your own state standards.

Chapters 2 through 7 center on Bloom's Taxonomy (Bloom et al., 1956), a pyramidal structure that proceeds from the simple to the complex, whether we are looking at measurable objectives, paper-and-pencil tests, performance-based assessments, or portfolios. We demonstrate how the teaching of higher-order thought processes is much more effective when proceeding from a baseline level.

Chapter 2 exemplifies how objectives may be written within a cognitive hierarchy that describes simple to complex thought processes that can be applied to any subject area. These daily formative assessments lead to summative assessments through major paper-and-pencil tests (Chapters 3, 4 and 5) and performance-based projects (Chapter 6), which may be appropriately categorized in your students' portfolios (Chapter 7). Just as instructional objectives proceed from the simple to the complex via the Taxonomy, so should the items on paper-and-pencil tests. Hence, the chapters focusing on true–false, completion, multiple-choice, matching, short-answer, and essay items demonstrate how to write these items within appropriate levels of the Taxonomy. You and your students together can place them in their portfolios according to taxonomic level.

We advocate that you organize the contents of your tests in ascending order of difficulty: They should be "steeply graded" (Kubiszyn & Borich, 2007, p. 220), progressing from relatively easy to increasingly difficult items. We recommend this format for several reasons. First, such a format enhances student confidence. If the students first encounter a series of items that they can easily answer, they are more confident when taking on the more difficult items that come later. In addition, they do not become frustrated and fatigued to the point that they miss some of the easier items that they would have answered correctly had they been placed at the beginning of the format. Hence, a simple-to-complex format is recommended in both formative and summative assessment.

Before issuing report cards, we suggest that you and your students categorize representative evidence of their formative and summative performances within their portfolios according to the cognitive hierarchy (discussed in Chapter 7). A careful review of student artifacts should enhance the quality of your instruction by highlighting the students' strengths as well as their weaknesses.

The core of this book is a combination of thorough explanations and abundant examples to guide you through the steps of our model of instruction and assessment that proceeds from a Knowledge-level baseline through the echelons of higher-order thinking processes within the cognitive domain. The daily objectives are the essence of continual, formative assessment and progress from the Knowledge to the Evaluation levels of Bloom's Taxonomy (Bloom et al., 1956). Writing measurable daily instructional objectives for progressive pupil performance through each of the cognitive levels allows you to detect student and instructional strengths, as well as weaknesses, within each level. As conduits of measurable assessment, these objectives provide for the reinforcement of effective teaching strategies, while simultaneously enabling you to ameliorate student weaknesses by reviewing, redirecting, or adjusting current instructional strategies; creating new strategies; or implementing materials that are commensurate with your students' needs.

Ideally, this type of planning and assessment should be supported throughout a school district, beginning with the superintendent and continued by the curriculum director, building principals, teacher leaders, teachers, and paraprofessionals. Such an effort would optimize student learning per se and also maximize student performance on statewide assessments (more about this in Chapter 1).

At the beginning of each chapter, we furnish you with easy-to-follow diagrams that show where we are, where we have been, and where we are going. In addition, to provide you with firsthand involvement with our method, each chapter ends with a section called Professional Development Activities. These activities further your expertise in the design of your personal instruction and assessment practices. They could also be a part of virtually any inservice session.

1 Deconstructing the Standards

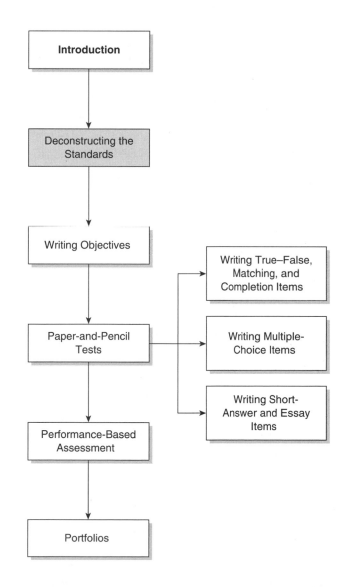

Introduction

↓

Deconstructing the Standards

Bloom's Taxonomy

Knowledge

Comprehension

Application

Analysis

Synthesis

Evaluation

↓

Writing Objectives

↓

Paper-and-Pencil Tests → Writing True–False, Matching, and Completion Items

Paper-and-Pencil Tests → Writing Multiple-Choice Items

↓

Performance-Based Assessment → Writing Short-Answer and Essay Items

↓

Portfolios

Much of the academic curriculum in today's schools is dictated by the respective state standards, which are frequently based on national standards, such as those from the *Principles and Standards for School Mathematics*, the *National Science Education Standards*, the *National Standards for Social Studies Teachers*, and the *Standards for the English Language Arts*. However, it is often difficult to translate these standards into practical classroom implications because of confusion generated by their broad generality and the absence of sufficient direction for their implementation. Hence teachers often have a negative view of standards per se.

Our goal in this chapter is to help you modify the wording of any standard into performance terminology and then transmit it into unit plan and daily instructional objectives, all within a progressive sequence of specificity. This sequence can serve as a set of blueprints for classroom instruction. As you know, most reputable contractors would not consider building a house without blueprints. Of course, changes may occur after construction has begun, but not without accompanying changes in the blueprints, because they provide a basis for ongoing (formative) and conclusive (summative) assessment, and they also enable the contractor to determine whether corrections are in order. Instructional objectives serve the same purpose for classroom instruction.

The litmus test for any instructional objective is whether it provides for objective assessment. Hence clear language and specific intent should be inherent in every objective at every level. Of course, the level of specificity should increase from national standards to unit plan objectives to daily instructional objectives, and clarity of intent should be vividly present throughout.

Some measurement specialists caution against overadhering to specificity in instructional objectives, fearing that teachers may spend a disproportionate amount of time writing objectives at the expense of preparing for instruction (e.g., Popham, 1995, p. 80). We believe that this is an unwarranted fear.

As we mentioned in the Introduction, virtually all statewide assessment tests are based on state standards, which stem from the national standards. These high-stakes tests are criterion referenced, and aligning your lesson plans with them using our process can certainly enhance your students' performance on these critical examinations: Your comfort in implementing the standards into your instruction and assessment will result in higher student scores.

WRITING INSTRUCTIONAL OBJECTIVES FOR NATIONAL STANDARDS

We begin with sample items drawn from the national standards of the major content areas, break them down to behavioral terms, and transfer them into unit and finally, daily instructional objectives. This conversion process can be easily applied to the standards of any particular state. We now demonstrate this process for each of the major content areas.

Mathematics

Many of the examples used here are paraphrased or taken directly from the *Principles and Standards for School Mathematics* (National Council of Teachers of Mathematics, 2000). This important document, originally released in 1989 by the National Council of Teachers of Mathematics (NCTM), has been adopted in most states. The following example is taken from the Algebra Standard for Grades 6–8, a verbatim portion of the actual standard.

National Standard

Use mathematical models to represent and understand quantitative relationships.

This standard is relatively clear and accessible. However, we can make it more meaningful by including observable evidence of the students' abilities.

Modified National Standard

Students will evidence the ability to use mathematical models to represent and understand quantitative relationships.

We use the term *evidence* to indicate that students must show that they have met predetermined criteria for fulfilling the standard through observable behaviors. This term is used again in the unit plan objective for continuity and to ensure the observable proof that students are able to use mathematical models to represent and understand quantitative relationships.

Unit Plan Objective

Students will evidence the ability to use graphs, charts, and diagrams to show the relationship between various units of distance and volume.

As you can see, this unit plan objective includes the original standard while providing for a diversity of means for its fulfillment through daily instructional objectives. The following objective illustrates how a high level of specificity can still include the components of the original standard.

Daily Instructional Objective

Presented with a chart displaying six different distances in yards, the students will shade in the metric equivalent of each, with a 1/10 margin of error.

Adhering to the unit plan objective, this daily instructional objective is specific in terms of media ("a chart displaying six different distances in yards"), observable behavior ("shade"), and minimal standards of performance ("with a 1/10 margin of error"). Through this specificity, it provides a means for addressing the task dictated by the original standard, the modified standard, and unit plan objective. Remember, this daily instructional objective is but one component within the unit plan that is directed toward the achievement of the national standard.

Science

As with any other discipline taught in Grades K–12, adherence to the respective state standards or *National Science Education Standards* is imperative for any teacher of science. Let us demonstrate how broad national and state science standards can be stated in specific terms appropriate for unit and daily objectives.

Here is a progression using an actual standard as prescribed in the 5–8 Content F, Science in Personal and Social Perspectives from the National Research Council's (1996) *National Science Education Standards*.

National Standard

All students should develop understanding of personal health, populations, resources, environments, natural hazards, risks and benefits, and science and technology in society.

The complex and disjointed content of this standard makes translation into a single and understandable modified standard difficult—a standard like this makes clear why teachers often view standards negatively. However, these translations are easily possible when you follow our steps of conversion. Here is an example of how to deconstruct such standards into logical and understandable guidelines for instruction.

Modified National Standard

Students will demonstrate an understanding of the interrelationships among personal health, populations, resources, environments, natural hazards, risks and benefits, and science and technology in society.

The verb *demonstrates* is a precursor of observable pupil performance in the forthcoming objectives. Then the term *interrelationships* serves as a connector that brings the disjointed components of the original standard into an understandable whole while still providing for a plethora of unit plan objectives, such as the following.

Unit Plan Objective

Students will demonstrate an understanding of the interrelationships between the personal health of the members of urban environments and those from rural environments within the eastern section of the United States.

In adherence to the modified standard, this objective uses the verb *demonstrate* and then specifies and refines some of the previously mentioned relationships. As shown in the following daily instructional objective, you can use a variety of specific activities for meeting the goal dictated by the national standard and refined by this unit plan objective.

Daily Instructional Objective

Following a class discussion and an out-of-class reading assignment, students will list three similarities and three differences between the general health of urban residents over the age of 55 and that of their rural counterparts.

Continuing the pattern of increasing specificity, this daily instructional objective is detailed in its partial fulfillment of the original standard. It specifies how the students are to engage in the observable behavior ("list"), and it is clear in stating exactly what is expected ("three similarities and three differences"). Again, however, this is only one in a series of daily instructional objectives that can be used to meet the prescribed national standard.

Social Studies

In 1994, the National Council for the Social Studies released ten broad strands that became the basis for the subsequently published national standards. As dictated by the *National Standards for Social Studies Teachers* (NCSS) Volume 1 (1997), social studies is not a single discipline but rather a multidimensional collection that encompasses virtually all of the social science disciplines. Understandably, such a broad sweep can be intimidating to teachers who may be puzzled as how to transfer these overarching standards to unit plans and daily instructional objectives in a comprehensible and measurable progression. In the following example based on one of the NCSS standards, we provide direction for an easy and understandable progression through this sequence.

National Standard

Geography: High School Teacher Expectations

Enable learners to describe the process, patterns, and functions of human settlement.

Written in terms of teacher actions, this standard is easily transmitted into pupil performance.

Modified National Standard

Students will describe the processes, patterns, and functions of human settlement.

While maintaining the literal components of the original standard, the modified standard puts it into student behaviors that can become progressively more specific with the unit and daily instructional objectives. We begin this progression with the following unit plan objective.

Unit Plan Objective

Students will select an ethnic group, explain some of the reasons for its movement across the country, and describe specific influences it has had on regional cultures during its migration.

As a refined extension of the original and modified standards, this unit plan objective specifies students' focus. Although much more specific than the original and the modified standards, the openness of this unit plan objective provides for a multiplicity of daily instructional objectives, such as the following.

Daily Instructional Objective

Continuing individual in-class research projects, students will use the library and Internet to select an ethnic group, determine its U.S.

point of origin, provide at least one reason for its movement, trace its state-by-state journey, and include at least three influences that this group has had on regional cultures, for inclusion in a three- to five-page report.

This objective carries the original standard to a high level of specificity. Although it allows students their choice of ethnic groups to research, it states precisely what is to be covered in the report: the U.S. point of origin, at least one reason for the group's movement, its state-by-state journey, at least three influences it has had on regional cultures, and the length of the report. Such detail provides the students with an understandable explanation of the requirements of the report, and it also serves as the basis for a set of rubrics, the criteria upon which the papers will be assessed (more about rubrics in Chapter 5).

English–Language Arts

The following example is taken word for word from Standard Eight of *The Standards for the English Language Arts* (National Council of Teachers of English and International Reading Association, 1996).

National Standard

Students use a variety of technological and information resources (e.g., libraries, databases, computer networks, video) to gather and synthesize information and to create and communicate knowledge.

This standard is especially broad and sweeping, devoid of restrictions or guidelines, giving practically unlimited options to the teacher regarding what to teach. Students are given equal freedom in their choice of resources.

Modified National Standard

Students will use a variety of information resources to gather and synthesize data and to create and communicate knowledge.

The redundancy of the original standard increases its ambiguity. Our shortening of it enhances its clarity.

Unit Plan Objective

Since the original standard and the modified standard have no content boundaries, the following unit plan objective focuses on a sample objective that adheres to the use of information resources.

Students will use printed and technological resources to research selected topics from the Elizabethan era.

Far more specific than the loosely written standards, this unit plan objective still provides for a variety of daily instructional objectives. The lone dictates are that the students must use both printed and technological resources, and their topics must pertain to the Elizabethan era.

Daily Instructional Objective

Continuing a series of in-class projects conducted within small cooperative groups, students will use printed and technological resources to gather basic information preparatory to constructing a four- to six-page report for an eight- to ten-minute class presentation on a self-selected topic pertaining to the Elizabethan era.

We have used a high degree of specificity here, in compliance with the mandates of the original standard, which are to use "technological and informational resources" and "to gather and synthesize information and to create and communicate knowledge." This series of daily instructional objectives directs the students to use printed and technological resources to amass information that they will use in subsequent days to write papers to be presented to the class.

SUMMARY

In this chapter, we have taken you through the process that can connect and align the national standards, the unit plans, and daily instructional objectives in the major content areas. Like an engineer or an architect, you, the teacher are allowed virtual freedom within predetermined guidelines. Your guidelines are the national or state standards and the ensuing unit plan objectives, and your freedom is in your creative construction and implementation of your daily instructional objectives. Like the engineer and the architect, however, your daily instructional objectives should be specific and measurable.

PROFESSIONAL DEVELOPMENT ACTIVITIES

Make certain that you have a copy of the state standards for the course or courses that you teach. Then break into groups of four or five according to subjects taught.

Together, select a standard and copy it verbatim. Next, modify it by making it more understandable and student focused. Be sure to include an action verb (e.g., *demonstrate*) as a precursor of the description of student performance in your unit and daily instructional objectives. Remember not to change the content of the original standard by deleting from or adding to it.

Keeping in mind that a number of unit plan objectives can stem from a modified standard, cooperatively construct a unit plan objective from any part of your modified standard. Be sure to use at least one action verb and present a general description of what you will expect of your students. You can use the content area samples in the chapter as templates.

Next, construct a daily instructional objective, selecting a portion of your unit plan objective (always remembering that many daily instructional objectives constitute one unit plan objective).

Be sure to include an action verb depicting observable pupil performance and mention configuration (e.g., in groups of three or four) and context or preparation (e.g., presented with an unlabeled diagram). Also, it is very important to specify exactly what you expect of your students (e.g., with an error margin of plus or minus five miles).

After you have completed this process, each group can put its four components (national standard, modified standard, unit plan objective, and daily instructional objective) on the board or on the overhead for discussion.

2 Writing Unit and Daily Instructional Objectives

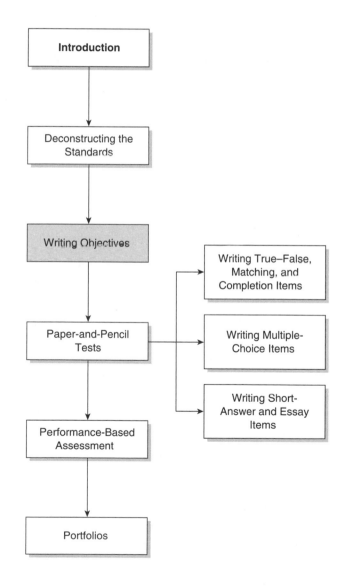

Introduction

↓

Deconstructing the Standards

↓

Bloom's Taxonomy

Knowledge
Comprehension
Application
Analysis
Synthesis
Evaluation

Writing Objectives

→ Writing True–False, Matching, and Completion Items

↓

Paper-and-Pencil Tests

→ Writing Multiple-Choice Items

→ Writing Short-Answer and Essay Items

↓

Performance-Based Assessment

↓

Portfolios

As we've demonstrated in Chapter 1, in essence, daily instructional objectives are the measurable means through which the general goals of the state standards and unit plan objectives are accomplished. As we've said, **Unit plan objectives** involve general goals, whereas **daily instructional objectives** are measurable, focused and specific.

When you write unit plan objectives, using terms such as *understanding*, *comprehension*, and so forth is fine, but only when coupled with performance terms (e.g., "demonstrate") or precursors of them (e.g., "evidence"):

The student will *demonstrate* understanding by . . .

The student will *evidence* comprehension of the task by . . .

By including a performance term, the unit plan objective sets the tone for the clear, specific, and measurable dictates of the daily instructional objective. Some authors (e.g., Kubiszyn & Borich, 2003) recommend that these objectives contain three components:

1. An observable student *behavior*

2. The *conditions* under which the behavior is expected to occur

3. *Minimal standards* of acceptable performance

Example: On a worksheet containing ten four-digit addition problems (*conditions*), the student will solve (*behavior*) at least eight of them (*minimal standards*).

Conditions are important components of daily instructional objectives. However, observable student behaviors and minimal standards of performance are virtually indispensable, because they provide the baseline for determining whether the objectives have been achieved.

Unit and daily instructional objectives can be structured for student involvement in activities that span the entire spectrum of any hierarchical model, thus providing a structure for the teaching of higher-order thinking skills. And engaging in higher-order thought processes is essential to maximum student learning.

Bloom et al.'s (1956) hierarchical model of the cognitive domain is widely used, and because of its relative simplicity and general familiarity, we have employed it as our reference point. Commonly referred to as Bloom's Taxonomy, it is a solid, pyramidal structure that provides for simple-to-complex thought processes within any content area. It is pyramidal in that each level is dependent on the previous levels. A firm knowledge baseline establishes the solidity of each successive level. Thus ascent through the sequence of higher-order thinking skills becomes a smooth and fluid passage for practically any student within any content area.

Here is a summary of Bloom's Cognitive Domain:

Summary of Bloom's Basic Cognitive Domain

1. KNOWLEDGE:	Recognition and recall of previously learned information; no comprehension or understanding of the information is implied
2. COMPREHENSION	The ability to understand or summarize information, translating information from one form or level to another, predicting continuations in trends of data
3. APPLICATION	The ability to take information that has previously been acquired and comprehended and use it in concrete situations
4. ANALYSIS	The ability to break down a unified whole into its basic parts and understand the relationship among these parts, determining cause–effect relationships, understanding analogies and metaphor, determining classifications
5. SYNTHESIS	The assemblage of parts into a new whole, the formulation of a new hypothesis or plan of action, constructing a solution to an unfamiliar problem
6. EVALUATION	The ability to judge a phenomenon on the basis of predetermined criteria or internal consistency

To show the progression through the Taxonomy, we take the words from a simple vocabulary test and demonstrate how they can be used to determine performance within each of the six levels of this cognitive hierarchy. (Such a progression can be used with any content area, as we've mentioned.)

Knowledge Level: A ten-item written quiz on which students define each of the words is a Knowledge-level activity because it involves only rote memorization.

Comprehension Level: Students writing any synonyms not talked about in class for each of their vocabulary words is a Comprehension-level activity because they are translating the words' meanings from one form to another.

Application Level: Students correctly using each of their ten vocabulary words in separate written sentences is an Application-level activity because they are taking information that has been acquired or comprehended and using it in a concrete situation.

Analysis Level: Students splitting each of their ten words into syllables on a written exercise is an Analysis-level activity because they are breaking a unified whole into its basic parts; to do this, they must understand the relationship among the parts.

Synthesis Level: Students correctly using each of their ten words in a creative story is a Synthesis-level activity because they are assembling parts into a new whole.

Evaluation Level: Students writing three reasons why they thought a particular assignment was or was not worthwhile is an Evaluation-level activity because they are making value judgments on the basis of personal, experiential criteria.

CONTENT AREAS AND COGNITIVE DOMAIN LEVELS

Mathematics

Knowledge Level: Students can recognize and recall previously learned information; no comprehension or understanding of the information is implied.

Both the unit and the daily instructional objectives should indicate that at this level, the students are expected only to demonstrate the ability to recall previously learned information. For example, many mathematical processes—both simple and complex—are dependent on the knowledge of formulae, and you probably require your students to memorize formulae to determine area.

Unit Plan Instructional Objective

Example: Students will evidence knowledge of formulae for areas.

In using the term *knowledge,* this unit plan objective indicates that student performance is to occur at the Knowledge level: The students must demonstrate that they can recall previously introduced information. The assertion that students *evidence knowledge* leads to the measurable specificity that characterizes the following sample daily instructional objective.

Daily Instructional Objective

> On a worksheet containing the names of five geometrical figures, students will write the formula for computing the area of each.

Writing the formulae for determining areas of geometrical figures is a Knowledge-level activity involving memorization. The objective clearly and succinctly describes the conditions ("On a worksheet containing the names of five geometrical figures"), behavior ("write"), and minimal standards of acceptable performance ("the formula for computing the area of each").

Comprehension Level: Students are able to understand or summarize information, translate information from one form or level to another, and comprehend data trends.

During the early stages of a unit on statistics, you probably explain how specific statistical techniques can provide answers to given problems. At this stage, your students would not be required to apply these techniques, only to select those that are applicable to the solutions of such problems.

Unit Plan Instructional Objective

> Students will express understanding of formulae appropriate for solving specific types of problems.

This is a Comprehension-level objective in that it goes beyond the simple memorization of formulae without requiring their application. Then it points to later performance in the daily instructional objectives by stating that the students "will express understanding."

Daily Instructional Objective

> On a worksheet containing five descriptive statistical problems, the students will write the formulae for computing each in the provided spaces.

In this objective, the students must express more than the memorization of formulae, but they are not required to apply this knowledge. They are instructed to demonstrate comprehension of the formulae by writing each beside a problem where the solution is dependent on that particular formula. The objective is also clear in its individual requirements: conditions ("In the provided spaces on a worksheet containing five descriptive statistical problems"), behavior ("write"), and minimal standards ("the formulae for computing each").

Application Level: Students have the ability to take information that has previously been acquired and comprehended and use it in concrete situations.

After introducing the formulae for specific statistical computations, you may decide to assess your students' ability to apply these formulae by presenting them with a set of numbers with which they could perform given statistical computations.

Unit Plan Instructional Objective

> Students will use statistical formulae appropriate for solving problems of central tendency.

The term *use* is synonymous with *apply*. Hence, students are expected to apply previously learned formulae in the concrete situations of solving problems of central tendency.

Daily Instructional Objective

> Given fifty random numbers, students will compute their mean and median to two decimal places.

Means and medians are computed by the application of formulae, which makes this an Application-level objective. The conditions are distinct ("Given fifty random numbers"), as are the behavior ("compute"), and the minimal standards of acceptable performance ("the mean and the median to two decimal places").

Analysis Level: Students are able to break a unified whole into its basic parts and understand the relationship among those parts, compare and contrast phenomena, understand metaphors and analogies, understand the relationship between cause and effect, and categorize phenomena.

Here is a sample unit plan objective to assist your students in understanding mathematical relationships:

Unit Plan Instructional Objective

> Students will demonstrate the ability to determine the subsets of intersecting sets.

Determining subsets at the points of set intersections is an Analysis-level exercise. The term *demonstrate* is a prelude to the observable behaviors delineated in ensuing daily instructional objectives.

Daily Instructional Objective

> Presented with three intersecting sets, students will correctly list each set's subsets.

To meet this objective, students must understand relationships among the sets, an Analysis-level exercise. The conditions ("Presented with three intersecting sets"), the behavior ("list"), and the minimal standards of performance ("correctly list each of the subsets of the intersecting sets") are all present. The purpose of the term *correctly* is to indicate that *only* each of the subsets is to be listed.

Synthesis Level: Students are able to assemble parts into a whole, formulate new hypotheses or plans of action, and construct solutions to unfamiliar problems.

To promote mathematical creativity, you can ask your students to take geometrical formulae that they have acquired and comprehended and apply them imaginatively.

Unit Plan Instructional Objective

> Students will use geometrical formulae in the creative design of various structures.

Prescribing the creative application of previously acquired and comprehended formulae is a Synthesis-level objective. Also, the term *use* connotes observable pupil behavior.

Daily Instructional Objective

> In groups of two or three, students will use at least four geometrical formulae in drawing plans for the construction of the shell of a building twenty feet by forty feet, including a roof, gutters, and two rainspouts.

In this objective, students are encouraged to be creative within a given parameter. This does not stifle their creativity; it fosters it within a dimension that they may not have discovered without guidance. Cooperative group work can also serve as a catalyst to creativity. The objective delineates conditions ("In groups of two or three"), behaviors ("use," "drawing"), and minimal standards ("the construction of the shell of a building twenty feet by forty feet . . .").

Evaluation Level: Students are able to make value judgments on the basis of predetermined criteria or internal consistency. Since value judgments often involve personal choices, you should assess the students' rationale for their decisions as opposed to their decisions per se.

Virtually all theorems lend themselves to various methods of proof. As in the following example, you can present theorems to your students and ask them to select a method of proof for each and justify its application.

Unit Plan Instructional Objective

Example: Students will choose methods of proof to apply to given theorems.

Based on student selectivity ("choose"), this is an Evaluation-level objective. Although the term *apply* is indicative of Application-level behavior, the students' selection of proofs elevates the objective into the Evaluation level, as a matter of choice.

Daily Instructional Objective

Given five theorems, students will select a method of proof (direct, contrapositive, or contradictory) to apply to each and list two reasons for each of their choices.

An Evaluation assignment in that the selection of the proofs is based on each student's personal criteria, this objective is specific in its intended conditions ("Given five theorems"), behaviors ("select," "apply," "list"), and minimal standards: conditions ("two reasons for each of their choices").

Science

Knowledge Level: Students can recognize and recall previously learned information; no comprehension or understanding of the information is implied.

Since knowledge of chemical symbols is elemental to student involvement in chemical processes and procedures, the following example targets the memorization of the symbols.

Unit Plan Instructional Objective

Students will reflect knowledge of chemical symbols.

Demonstrating knowledge of chemical symbols simply involves the display of previously memorized material. The term *demonstrate* indicates an observable student performance, as shown in the following daily instructional objective example.

Daily Instructional Objective

> On a ten-item quiz, students will write the corresponding symbol beside at least eight of the chemical elements.

This is an assignment involving rote memorization, which occurs at the Knowledge level. Performance oriented ("write"), the objective is definite with respect to its conditions ("On a ten-item quiz") and minimal standards ("at least eight").

Comprehension Level: Students are able to understand or summarize information, translate information from one form or level to another, and comprehend data trends.

To determine whether your students have a general understanding of a given demonstration, you can ask them to summarize it, as in the following example.

Unit Plan Instructional Objective

> Students will demonstrate comprehension of observed laboratory demonstrations.

Although broad in its intent, this objective specifies that students must demonstrate comprehension skills. The following daily instructional objective is only one of many available vehicles for meeting this unit plan objective.

Daily Instructional Objective

> Following the observation of a laboratory demonstration, students will provide written summaries that include (a) each of the three pieces of equipment used and (b) the three-step process of the demonstration, in sequence.

This is a Comprehension-level objective, which requires students to summarize an observed activity. It is precise with respect to the conditions ("Following an observed laboratory demonstration"). The behavior (to "provide") in itself lacks precision; however, "a written summary" clarifies exactly how the students are to proceed. The objective also makes clear what should be included in the summary, thus stating the minimal standards of performance: "(a) each of the three pieces of equipment used and (b) the three-step process of the demonstration, in sequence."

Application Level: Students have the ability to take information that has previously been acquired and comprehended and use it in concrete situations.

Student familiarity with the functions and the applications of instruments for the solutions of problems in the science lab is important for their further learning in this area. The colorimeter is one of these instruments, which we use in the following example.

Unit Plan Instructional Objective

Students will use colorimeters to solve problems.

The terms *use* and *solve* indicate the Application-level activities that will be required in the daily instructional objectives.

Daily Instructional Objective

As a lab exercise, students will use colorimeters to determine the specific gravity of an unknown sample within 0.2 units.

This is a hands-on Application-level objective with clearly stated conditions ("As a lab exercise"), behaviors ("use," "determine"), and minimal standards of acceptable performance ("within 0.2 units").

Analysis Level: Students are able to break a unified whole into its basic parts and understand the relationship among those parts, compare and contrast phenomena, understand metaphors and analogies, understand the relationship between cause and effect, and categorize phenomena.

Comparing and contrasting phenomena is a form of diagnosing or analyzing. As in the next example, you may wish to give your students hands-on experiences in comparing and contrasting different rock types.

Unit Plan Instructional Objective

Students will distinguish among different rock types.

By distinguishing, the students are comparing and contrasting, an Analysis-level activity. Although the term *distinguish* is somewhat indicative of observable pupil performance, the ensuing daily instructional objectives should clarify exactly how the student is to do this.

Daily Instructional Objective

When presented with an igneous and a metamorphic rock, students will list two similarities and two differences between the two.

This Analysis-level objective involves hands-on examination as a means of comparing and contrasting two different kinds of rocks. Interpretation is unnecessary because of the clarity of conditions ("When presented with an igneous rock and a metamorphic rock"), expected behavior ("list"), and minimal standards of performance ("two similarities and two differences").

Synthesis Level: Students are able to assemble parts into a whole, formulate new hypotheses or plans of action, and construct solutions to unfamiliar problems.

For instance, in a unit on motion, you can assist your students in the creative construction of devices to implement some of the concepts that they have developed, as we demonstrate in the following examples.

Unit Plan Instructional Objective

> Students will investigate the construction of a device capable of projecting an object through an obstacle course without the assistance of electricity.

Virtually any investigation involves the formulation and testing of hypotheses, which are usually observable, Synthesis-level activities. Also, the many facets of the construction of the proposed device would be observable as well.

Daily Instructional Objective

> In pairs, the students will draw preliminary plans for the construction of a nonelectrical machine to provide nonstop movement of a marble through its maze.

This objective is geared toward opportunities for student creativity within a general framework, which serves as the objective's standards of performance. In addition, the conditions are precise ("In pairs"), as is the behavior ("draw"), and the minimal standards ("a nonelectrical machine to provide nonstop movement of a marble through its maze").

Evaluation Level: Students are able to make value judgments on the basis of predetermined criteria or internal consistency. Since value judgments often involve personal choices, you should assess the students' rationale for their decisions as opposed to their decisions per se.

Multiple controversies exist between those who would preserve the environment and those who would use it for industrial purposes. If you wish to engage your students in researching the points of view of both sides, the following examples could apply.

Unit Plan Instructional Objective

> Students will research controversial environmental stances for the purpose of making rational value judgments regarding these issues.

This Evaluation-level objective calls for students to make sound value judgments based either on predetermined criteria or on the internal consistency of a particular point of view.

Daily Instructional Objective

Following the reading of an article supporting drilling for oil in Alaska and another opposing such drilling, students will determine which side of the issue they favor and list three facts from one of the articles to support their respective positions.

This is an Evaluation-level objective in that it requires value judgments from the students, but these value judgments are to be objective as opposed to emotional because the objective clearly states that the students' positions are to be supported by "three facts from one of the articles." Also, the objective is definite with respect to conditions ("Following the reading of an article . . ."), behaviors ("determine," "list"), and minimal standards ("list three facts . . .").

Social Studies

Knowledge Level: Students can recognize and recall previously learned information; no comprehension or understanding of the information is implied.

During the early middle-school years, students are usually expected to be familiar with the names of the fifty states and their respective capitals, which is accomplished through rote memorization.

Unit Plan Instructional Objective

Students will exhibit knowledge of the fifty states and their respective capitals.

Using the word *knowledge* in this context conveys that this is a Knowledge-level objective, and the term *exhibit* calls for observable student behavior in the daily instructional objective.

Daily Instructional Objective

On a blank map, students will correctly label the fifty states and their respective capitals, with no more than ten spelling errors.

The word *label* connotes a Knowledge-level performance involving memorization. The objective is precise in its specification of conditions ("On a blank map"), student behavior ("correctly label"), and minimal standards of acceptable performance (" . . . no more than ten spelling errors").

Comprehension Level: Students are able to understand or summarize information, translate information from one form or level to another, and comprehend data trends.

To develop your students' ability to transfer information from one form to another, you could ask them to display the same data on different graphs, as in the following examples.

Unit Plan Instructional Objective

> Students will demonstrate the ability to represent data through different modes.

The objective instructs that the student "display" this ability in ensuing daily instructional objectives.

Daily Instructional Objective

> When presented with a chart showing Louisiana rice production for the past five years, students will display this same information on a line graph.

Transferring bar graph data to a line graph is translating information from one form to another, a Comprehension-level activity. The conditions are clearly described ("When presented with a bar graph . . ."). The behavior, *display,* is observable "on a line graph," and the minimal standards of "this same information" prescribe 100% accuracy.

Application Level: Students have the ability to take information that has previously been acquired and comprehended and use it in concrete situations.

Many teachers expect their students to be able to interpret maps and to construct them as well. The following unit plan can implement such expectations.

Unit Plan Instructional Objective

> Students will apply acquired cartography skills

With its application of previously acquired skills, this is an Application-level objective, with a built-in call for observable student behavior ("apply").

Daily Instructional Objective

> As an outdoor assignment, students will individually construct a map, with a legend, showing the distance between two predetermined locations on the school grounds, with a margin of error not exceeding five feet.

This objective takes classroom knowledge into outdoor application. It is detailed and clear in its three components: conditions ("As an outdoor assignment,"), behavior ("individually construct"), and minimal standards of acceptable performance ("a map, with a legend, showing the distance between two predetermined locations . . . , with a margin of error not exceeding five feet").

Analysis Level: Students are able to break a unified whole into its basic parts and understand the relationship among those parts, compare and contrast phenomena, understand metaphors and analogies, understand the relationship between cause and effect, and categorize phenomena.

To assist your students in learning that there are many similarities among seemingly different peoples, as well as unique differences, objectives like the following could apply.

Unit Plan Instructional Objective

> Students will demonstrate the ability to discern that there are both similarities and unique differences among the holidays celebrated by this nation's peoples.

To discern that there are both similarities and differences among the holidays celebrated by the nation's peoples, the students must first make comparisons and contrasts among the holidays. Then they are required to demonstrate these discernments by the daily instructional objectives.

Daily Instructional Objective

> Following separate readings on Christmas and Kwanzaa, the students will list at least three similarities and three differences between the two holidays.

Since students are acquainting themselves with the two holidays through separate reading sources, they must make comparative analyses to determine similarities and differences between the two, thus making this an Analysis-level objective. It is precise with respect to conditions ("Following separate readings on Christmas and Kwanzaa"), behavior ("list"), and minimal standards of acceptable performance ("at least three similarities and three differences").

Synthesis Level: Students are able to assemble parts into a whole, formulate new hypotheses or plans of action, and construct solutions to unfamiliar problems.

As part of their study of international conflicts, you may want to involve your students in the creation of proposals for resolving these conflicts, thus heightening their awareness of the possibilities for peace.

Unit Plan Instructional Objective

> Students will propose plans for resolving conflicts between nations.

Proposing a plan of virtually any sort necessitates a creative endeavor. The daily objectives direct how it is to be observable.

Daily Instructional Objective

> In groups of two or three, students will design a peace proposal, for class presentation, that involves at least three compromises between the Israelis and the Palestinians.

Designing a peace proposal is a Synthesis-level activity. Although providing for wide creativity, the objective remains firm in its stipulations for conditions ("In groups of two or three," "for class presentations"), behavior ("design"), and minimal standards ("at least three compromises . . .").

Evaluation Level: Students are able to make value judgments on the basis of predetermined criteria or internal consistency. Since value judgments often involve personal choices, you should assess the students' rationale for their decisions as opposed to their decisions per se.

Since controversy surrounds many appropriations of public monies, you can give your students opportunities to evaluate such appropriations in terms of their perceptions of their internal consistencies using objectives such as the following.

Unit Plan Instructional Objective

> Students will demonstrate the ability to evaluate appropriations of public funds.

An Evaluation-level objective, it requires that the students "demonstrate" this process, thus forecasting observable pupil behavior in the ensuing daily instructional objectives.

Daily Instructional Objective

> After reading a factual and objective account of the monies unequally budgeted for new band and new football uniforms, students will support or criticize the imbalance of the appropriations by listing at least three reasons for their positions.

This objective stipulates that students are to make value judgments that will be assessed on the strength of their reasoning. The objective is also clear in its statement of conditions ("After reading a factual and objective account . . ."), behaviors ("support," "criticize," "listing"), and minimal standards ("at least three reasons").

English–Language Arts

Knowledge Level: Students can recognize and recall previously learned information; no comprehension or understanding of the information is implied.

At the secondary level, students should become familiar not only with the titles of literary works but also with their respective authors. A Knowledge-level task involving memorization, this is a necessary link to the later study of literary selections and their writers.

Unit Plan Instructional Objective

> Students will exhibit knowledge of authors and their works.

Broad in its intent, this is a Knowledge-level assignment. The term *exhibit* conveys the necessity of specifying observable pupil performance in the ensuing daily instructional objectives.

Daily Instructional Objective

> On a ten-item matching exercise, students will match at least eight of ten authors previously discussed in class with their respective works.

This daily instructional objective example involves the rote memorization of factual information. Definite in its intent, the objective is specific in its conditions ("On a ten-item matching exercise"); behavior ("match"); and minimal standards of acceptable performance ("at least eight of ten authors with their respective works").

Comprehension Level: Students are able to understand or summarize information, translate information from one form or level to another, and comprehend data trends.

Since synonyms are different forms of the same words, you can elevate a weekly vocabulary quiz to the Comprehension level by having your students write synonyms for the words without the assistance of a dictionary.

Unit Plan Instructional Objective

Students will display an understanding of synonyms.

The term *understanding* is a synonym for comprehension, thus identifying this as a Comprehension-level activity. To make sure that it is demonstrable, the objective states that the "students will display."

Daily Instructional Objective

Presented with ten familiar words, students will write two synonyms for each.

According to our definition, a component of comprehension is "translating information from one form or level to another," which is the essence of synonyms. Hence, the listing of synonyms is a Comprehension-level activity. The objective is precise in its conditions ("Presented with ten familiar words"), behavior ("write"), and standards of performance ("two synonyms for each").

Application Level: Students have the ability to take information that has previously been acquired and comprehended and use it in concrete situations.

Following an introduction of sentence types, you can determine your students' ability to apply their understanding by asking them to write examples of each type.

Unit Plan Instructional Objective

Students will demonstrate the ability to write the major types of sentences correctly.

By requiring students to write particular types of sentences, you are instructing them to apply information that has been acquired and comprehended.

Daily Instructional Objective

As a written assignment, students will construct a declarative, an interrogative, and an imperative sentence, with a total of no more than two mechanical or grammatical errors.

Writing these sentences is applying information that has previously been acquired (knowing the definitions of the sentences) and comprehended (understanding their characteristics and when to use them) in a concrete situation. The objective is straightforward with respect to its conditions ("As a written assignment"), behavior ("construct," which is observable since it is "a written assignment"), and minimal standards ("a declarative, an interrogative, and an imperative sentence, with a total of no more than two mechanical or grammatical errors").

Analysis Level: Students are able to break a unified whole into its basic parts and understand the relationship among those parts, compare and contrast phenomena, understand metaphors and analogies, understand the relationship between cause and effect, and categorize phenomena.

To enhance your students' understanding and enjoyment of literature, you can assist them in deciphering literary components, such as plot, theme, and symbolism, using objectives like the following:

Unit Plan Instructional Objective

Students will demonstrate the ability to decipher literary components of a novel.

The term *decipher* is indicative of Analysis-level performance in that it involves analyzing, investigating, or interpreting as opposed to translating. The objective also mandates that students "demonstrate" this ability.

Daily Instructional Objective

Upon completion of an assigned novel, students will explain, within three pages, the plot, two uses of symbolism, rising action, the climax, and falling action.

This is an Analysis-level assignment because none of the literary components is specifically identified or explained by name, thus necessitating an analytic investigation by the students. The objective itself, however, is clear and precise: conditions ("Upon completion of an assigned novel"), behavior ("explain"), and minimal standards ("within three pages: the plot, two uses of symbolism").

Synthesis Level: Students are able to assemble parts into a whole, formulate new hypotheses or plans of action, and construct solutions to unfamiliar problems.

To encourage your students to involve themselves in the writing of poetry, guidelines can assist them, while simultaneously serving as standards.

Unit Plan Instructional Objective

Students will engage in the writing of various poetry forms.

Synthesis-level in that it calls for the students to become involved in a creative process, the objective foretells the presence of standards in the ensuing daily instructional objectives because adherence to a poetry form (e.g., iambic pentameter, haiku) necessitates meeting a standard.

Daily Instructional Objective

As a class assignment, students will write a haiku about spring.

Writing an original haiku is a creative process with built-in standards: its seventeen-syllable form and the requirement that the poem be about spring. The conditions are also precise ("As a class assignment"), as is the behavior ("write").

Evaluation Level: Students are able to make value judgments on the basis of predetermined criteria or internal consistency. Since value judgments often involve personal choices, you should assess the students' rationale for their decisions as opposed to their decisions per se.

To assist your students in assessing the literary skills of the different writers they may encounter, you can guide them in arriving at objective evaluations through using objectives like the following:

Unit Plan Instructional Objective

Students will exhibit the ability to evaluate the literary skills of specific authors.

With the inclusion of the term *evaluate*, this is an Evaluation-level objective, and the term *exhibit* prescribes that the evaluation be observable.

Daily Instructional Objective

After reading a selection by Caldwell, students will explain, in a two- to three-page narrative, whether they agree with the author's treatment of poor, Southern, rural whites, containing at least three supporting reasons for their choices.

The requirement that the students evaluate a literary selection makes this an Evaluation-level objective. Although the objective allows for value judgments, it is precise in its structure of conditions ("After reading a selection by

Caldwell"), behavior ("explain"), and minimal standards ("a two- to three-page narrative . . . containing at least three supporting reasons").

SUMMARY

We have demonstrated that the unit plan, although somewhat general, conveys what should be accomplished in the subsequent daily instructional objectives, which should definitely be highly specific in its conditions, behaviors, and minimal standards of performance. They should eliminate any need for translation: They should be explicitly clear to students, teachers, parents, and curriculum directors. The conditions should describe when, where, or under what circumstances a particular behavior should occur, the behavior should be observable, and the minimal standards should be measurable.

We have demonstrated the importance of the sequential simple-to-complex structure of Bloom's pyramidal Taxonomy and how an understanding and acceptance of the dependency of each level on the previous levels make for a smooth ascent through the complexities of the higher-order thinking skills of any content area.

PROFESSIONAL DEVELOPMENT ACTIVITIES

In groups of three to five members, write unit plan objectives for the Knowledge level for your subject matter area. Be sure to include a precursor ("demonstrate," "evidence," "reflect," etc.) that indicates the observable performance that will be specified in the daily instructional objective. Make certain that your unit plan objective does not have the high level of specificity that will characterize your daily instructional objective.

From your unit plan objective, construct your daily instructional objective. Here, clarity of intent is very important. This objective must be vividly clear, devoid of any need for interpretation. Include the three components (behavior, conditions, and minimal standards), but be succinct, remembering that wordiness serves only to confuse. The conditions will describe when or where a particular behavior is to take place. For this behavior, use an action verb, one that can be observed. Last, your standards of acceptable performance should be easily measurable. For example, do not specify that the students will recite 80% of the alphabet; this is meaningless. Instead, specify that they will recite the alphabet in sequence with no more than two errors.

When you have completed the assignment, put it on the board or overhead for discussion. Then do the same thing for Comprehension, Application, Analysis, Synthesis, and Evaluation.

WWW RESOURCES

http://www.gsu.edu/~mstmbs/CrsTools/Magerobj.html
This Web site of George Mason University gives a synopsis of Mager's approach to the writing of instructional objectives.

http://edtech.tennessee.edu/~bobannon/
This Web site of The University of Tennessee is an online module designed to assist preservice teachers in developing unit and lesson plans that guide instruction in K–12 classrooms.

http://edweb.sdsu.edu/courses/EDTEC540/objectives/Objectives Home.html
This Web site of San Diego State University proffers techniques for writing valid instructional objectives that are commensurate with given problems.

3 Writing True–False and Completion Items and Matching Exercises

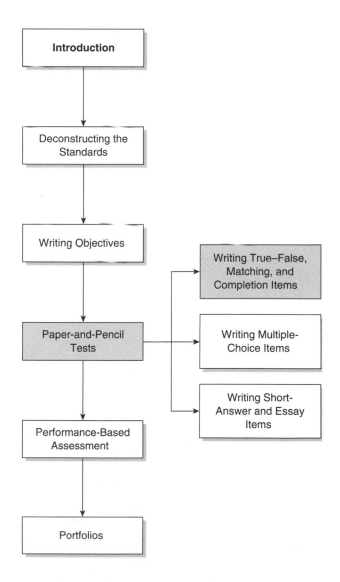

Introduction

Deconstructing the Standards

Bloom's Taxonomy
Knowledge
Comprehension
Application
Analysis
Synthesis
Evaluation

Writing Objectives

Paper-and-Pencil Tests

Writing True–False, Matching, and Completion Items

Writing Multiple-Choice Items

Writing Short-Answer and Essay Items

Performance-Based Assessment

Portfolios

Your daily instructional objectives, which we discuss in Chapters 1 and 2, can serve as excellent baselines for your formative assessments. They can convey the daily progress of your students, and they can also alert you to any need to alter your teaching methods or pacing, thus contributing to your summative assessments.

Suzanne Fodor, a teacher from Slippery Rock, Pennsylvania, describes how daily instructional objectives allow for continual formative assessments, which in turn provide for adjustments in teaching methodologies that result in the enhancement of her students' academic performances:

> As an experienced teacher, I have learned the value of flexible planning and frequent, multiple assessments. Specifically, without such planning and assessments, I really would have no idea of whether the method or pace of my instruction is conducive to optimal student performance, or whether my selected means of assessment accurately convey my pupils' progress.
>
> When I was a new teacher, I had the tendency to cover too much material much too quickly. I once taught an entire unit on meteorology under the assumption that my students would study each day and then be ready for my summative assessment, which would come in the form of a unit test consisting entirely of multiple-choice items. From the disastrous results of this test, I immediately understood that if the students weren't learning, the teacher probably hadn't done a very good job of teaching.
>
> In reteaching this unit, my daily instructional objectives included frequent and multiple types of formative assessment, which allowed me to align my teaching methods with the learning rates and styles of my students. Then, instead of consisting exclusively of multiple-choice items, my unit test also included models that my students were both to draw and complete to demonstrate their understanding of the material. Undoubtedly, the results of this second unit test were more favorable to my students, as well as to me.
>
> As a teacher, I am like a health-care specialist engaged in preventative medicine. This medical specialist prescribes programs designed for the wellness of the patients, which is determined by their frequent checkups. These checkups, in turn, provide for continual adjustments in the patients' programs. Analogous to the health-care specialist, I design instructional objectives for the academic health of my students; and a variety of frequent, formal assessments allows me to make instructional adjustments directed toward the enhancement of my students' performance. (S. Fodor, personal communication, July 25, 2008)

Paper-and-pencil tests, which we discuss in depth in this chapter as well as Chapters 4 and 5, can serve as bases for both formative and summative assessments, as can the various types of performance-based activities described in Chapter 6 and the portfolio process described in Chapter 7.

THREE KINDS OF TEST ITEMS

True–False Items

The **true–false** test is an effective and economical instrument for measuring the acquisition of specific facts. Like the multiple-choice test, it provides for wide sampling in a relatively short period of time. Unlike the multiple-choice test, it is restricted in its measurement of higher-order thought processes. True–false tests can measure cognitive functions well at the Knowledge level and in some instances also at the Comprehension level within any content area, as we demonstrate.

Some test constructors have attempted to measure higher-level thought processes by designing a more sophisticated alternative to the standard true–false item. In this variation, students are asked to fill in a blank that will make a false statement true (Linn & Gronlund, 2000). Although items that are partially true and partially false have certain merit, they can be confusing and potentially interfere with maximum test performance. For this reason, we advocate essay or short-answer items for measuring higher-order thought processes. We recommend that true–false items be used primarily at the Knowledge level and sparingly at the Comprehension level.

Guidelines for Constructing True–False Questions

True–false items, like any other items, should be clear, precise, and understandable to students. They should be short, and concise, and contain one single thought free of ambiguities and contradictions. Box 3.1 gives you both poor and good examples.

Box 3.1

Poor Example:	George Washington, John Adams, Thomas Jefferson, Benjamin Franklin, and Abraham Lincoln each served as president of the United States.

With its inclusion of five names, this item is excessively long and confusing. Moreover, four of the names make it a true statement, whereas the name of Benjamin Franklin makes it a false statement.

Good Example:	Thomas Jefferson served as president of the United States.
Good Example:	Benjamin Franklin served as president of the United States.

An exception to the single-thought principle is the occasional use of a qualifying clause within an item. However, it should be remembered that qualifying clauses often indicate to the examinees that the item is true, regardless of whether they actually know the answer. Qualifiers such as "possibly," "often," and "occasionally" are usually indicators of true responses. Students learn to recognize that items that are proportionately longer also have a tendency to be true. Conversely, absolutes such as "every," "never," or "all" indicate to the students, very early in their academic careers, that the item is false. Also, many students easily recognize patterns such as TTFF, but these unintentional clues can be avoided through the random placement of correct responses, accomplished through the toss of a coin.

Completion or Fill-In-the-Blank Items

The **completion** item can be a highly objective medium for measuring the acquisition of factual information. However, to use it for measurement beyond the Knowledge level is asking it to do something it's not built to do. For example, you would not use a completion item to measure an Analysis-level achievement, such as knowing what characteristics are shared by birds and butterflies.

Remember, the completion item is considered to be an objective item; the foregoing example is not an objective item. Like this one, completion items are often misused and abused, to the confusion of the student. This confusion can be avoided if certain principles of construction are followed.

Guidelines for Constructing Completion Items

The answer blank should always be placed at the end of the item, not at the beginning and not in the middle. The reason is that the stem should clearly present a problem to be solved in the answer blank. If the blank is in the middle or at the beginning of the stem, or even worse, if there is more than one blank, the examinees are likely to waste considerable time and patience in attempting to determine exactly what is expected. With the stem forming a problem to be answered in the blank, students know what is expected of them. If they do not fill in the correct response, it is because they do not know the answer, not because they do not understand the problem. Box 3.2 gives examples.

Box 3.2

Bad Example: On July 1, 1863, the _____ began during the Civil War.

Good Example: The name of the Civil War battle that began on July 1, 1863, is the

_____ .

Another problem that many neophyte test constructors have with the completion item lies in devising items that provide for one and only one correct answer.

Box 3.3

Bad Example: Columbus first came to the New World in (<u>a boat, a hurry, etc.</u>).

Good Example: Columbus first came to the New World in the year <u>(1492).</u>

Although we do not want to confuse our students with the structure or wording of the item, we also do not want to give unintentional clues by the number of blank lines in the answer blank. Hence, there should be one uniform line for all of the completion items on the test, regardless of whether the item can be answered with a single word or date, or with a phrase or a list. Box 3.4 gives examples.

Box 3.4

Bad Example: The name of the author who wrote *Charlotte's Web* is _____ _____ _____ _____.

Good Example:
The name of the author who wrote *Charlotte's Web* is _____.

Bad Example: Patrick Henry is most noted for his phrase "_____ ___ _____ _____ ___ _____ ___ ____ ___."

Good Example:
Patrick Henry is most noted for his phrase "_____."

Bad Example: If the clothes you are wearing catch fire, you should _____, _____, and _____.

Good Example:
If the clothes you are wearing catch fire, you should _____.

The indefinite articles (*a* and *an*) should be excluded from the stem, as well as any numbers (see Box 3.5).

Box 3.5

Bad Example: The part of speech that names a person, place, or thing is a _____.

Good Example: The part of speech that names a person, place, or thing is _____.

(Continued)

(Continued)

Bad Example: The names of the three primary colors are _____.

Good Example: The names of the primary colors are _____.

In the two good examples, the indefinite article *a* and the number *three* are excluded. The absence of these two terms enables students to complete the item without the assistance of a hint or a clue.

The completion or fill-in-the-blank item lends itself to Knowledge-level testing in virtually all of the content areas in the general K–12 curriculum.

Matching Exercises

Because of its compact efficiency, the **matching exercise** can cover a broad latitude of associative information. It can measure a multiplicity of relationships between various phenomena. Although most of these associations are restricted to facts, they can extend into understanding, as defined at the Comprehension level, and even into categorization of data and determination of cause–effect relationships, at the Analysis level.

Guidelines for Constructing Matching Exercises

In a matching exercise, items that typically fall on the left-hand side of the page are called *premises,* such as the names of states. The items on the right-hand side are called *responses,* such as the names of the state capitals. The premises and responses should be homogenous to ensure the associative nature of the exercise, as in the following example:

Match the states with their capital cities.

___1. Louisiana	a. Austin
___2. Texas	b. Raleigh
___3. Pennsylvania	c. Baton Rouge
___4. Nevada	d. Harrisburg
___5. North Carolina	e. Las Vegas
	f. Carson City

As with any other test exercise, the format and wording of the matching exercise should be easy to understand. However, neither the wording nor the format should give clues to the correct response. As prevention against unintentional clues, the number of possible responses should be greater than the number of premises—as in the capital cities example. This narrows the probability that student will arrive at the correct answer through the process of elimination, as opposed to informed selection. However, an exception to this may occur in instances where responses may be used more than once; in such cases, the directions should specify that responses may be used more than once.

Linn and Miller (2005) contend that "There certainly should be no more than ten items in either column" (p. 183) to make instructional adjustments directed toward the enhancement of the students' performance. However, we feel that the number of premises should not be fewer than five or more than eight for elementary students, and no less than five and no more than ten for secondary students. Should you determine that more associations are necessary, fine; simply include more matching exercises. Make certain that each matching exercise is contained on one page; turning back and forth can cause students to lose their trains of thought.

For ease of understanding, both the premises (on the left) and the responses (on the right) should be brief, with the response items shorter—for instance, an event (left) and its date (right). The principle is analogous to that of the multiple-choice item, whose stem presents a problem (premise) that is solved by the correct option (response).

COGNITIVE LEVELS SUITABLE FOR THE THREE KINDS OF TEST ITEMS

For each cognitive level in each content area, we start with a brief statement of the defining characteristics of that level, as we did in Chapter 2.

True–False Items

Mathematics

Knowledge Level: Students can recognize and recall previously learned information; no comprehension or understanding of the information is implied.

True–false tests are an economical means for sampling your students' knowledge of memorized material—formulae, for instance.

   T The formula for computing the area of a square is $S \times S$ or S^2.

This is a Knowledge-level item in that the correct response is dependent on students' knowledge and recall. Structurally, the item is short, and to the point, and contains a single thought.

Comprehension Level: Students are able to understand or summarize information, translate information from one form or level to another, and comprehend data trends.

Comprehension of the commutative properties of equations is an important mathematical concept, and the true–false test can sample your students' understanding of such concepts.

_T_ $(9 \times 2) + 6 = (3 \times 4) \times 2$

Comprehension-level in that the student is required to understand that the two equations yield the same total, this item is succinct, direct, and easy to understand.

Science

Knowledge Level: Students can recognize and recall previously learned information; no comprehension or understanding of the information is implied.

Knowledge of chemical symbols is prerequisite to chemistry involvement, and you can effectively use the true–false test as a means of sampling your students' ability to recognize these symbols.

_F_ H_2O is the symbol for hydrogen.

Brief and direct, this item calls for simple recognition on the part of the student. Also, the item is clear, requires no interpretation, and contains a single thought.

Comprehension Level: Students are able to understand or summarize information, translate information from one form or level to another, and comprehend data trends.

A component of the Comprehension level is the demonstrated ability to understand information in its various forms; you can use the true–false item to determine the students' comprehension of the relationship between chromosomes and chromatids.

_T_ A chromatid is a type of chromosome.

According to the *American Heritage College Dictionary* (2002), a *chromatid* is: "either of two daughter strands of a duplicated chromosome joined by a single centromere." Hence, this item is designed to test the students' comprehension of the presence of a relationship. Moreover, the item is clear and distinct and contains a single thought, devoid of ambiguities.

Social Studies

Knowledge Level: Students can recognize and recall previously learned information; no comprehension or understanding of the information is implied.

Virtually any study of U.S. geography necessitates knowledge of the states' respective capitals. The true–false test is an economical means of sampling students' knowledge of these relationships.

_F_ Reno is the capital of Nevada.

Brief, clear, and to the point, this statement simply tests students' recognition of previously presented material.

Comprehension Level: Students are able to understand or summarize information, translate information from one form or level to another, and comprehend data trends.

Understanding the time period of a movie or written work is a Comprehension-level process. You can determine if your students understand the historical period upon which a classic film focuses with a true–false test item.

_F_ *Sergeant York* takes place during World War II.

Comprehension-level in that it requires generalization from the students, this item is terse, direct, and contains a single, noncontradictory point.

English–Language Arts

Knowledge Level: Students can recognize and recall previously learned information; no comprehension or understanding of the information is implied.

To determine whether your students can equate authors with their respective works, the true–false item is an acceptable vehicle.

_F_ Mark Twain is the author of *The Song of Hiawatha*.

Knowledge-level in that it requires demonstration of rote factual information, this item is terse and succinct and contains a single thought with no contradictions.

Comprehension Level: Students are able to understand or summarize information, translate information from one form or level to another, and comprehend data trends.

You can use a true–false item to discover students' comprehension of a book's geographical setting.

_F_ Most of *Tom Sawyer* takes place in Mississippi.

Testing students' understanding of *Tom Sawyer*'s setting, this is a Comprehension-level item. Moreover, it is brief and understandable and contains one thought.

Completion or Fill-in-the-Blank Items

Mathematics

Knowledge Level: Students can recognize and recall previously learned information; no comprehension or understanding of the information is implied.

The completion exercise is a good way to sample students' knowledge of their recollection of given formulas; for instance,

The formula for computing the area of a circle is _____ πr^2 _____.

This is a Knowledge-level item in that it presents a problem involving recall, which is solved in the answer blank.

Science

Knowledge Level: Students can recognize and recall previously learned information; no comprehension or understanding of the information is implied.

For example, a completion test samples students' knowledge of constellations very well.

The name of the constellation of which the Big Dipper is a part is _____ *Ursa Major* _____.

Involving rote memorization, this Knowledge-level item has a single answer blank on which two words are to be written. There is no danger of there being more than one correct answer, and no unintentional clues are given.

Social Studies

Knowledge Level: Students can recognize and recall previously learned information; no comprehension or understanding of the information is implied.

Remembering dates and events is a component of the Knowledge level. You can use the completion test to sample your students' knowledge in this area.

The complete date on which the Japanese bombed Pearl Harbor was _____*December 7, 1941*_____.

This is a Knowledge-level item in that it involves remembering a date. The answer blank is at the end of the item; there is no danger of there being more than one correct answer, as specified by the word *complete*; no clues are given in the stem; and a single, uniform line is supplied for the day, month, and year.

English–Language Arts

Knowledge Level: Students can recognize and recall previously learned information; no comprehension or understanding of the information is implied.

As a means of determining your students' knowledge of various forms of poetry, you can use the completion test, as follows.

The name of a seventeen-syllable form of poetry is _____*haiku*_____.

Knowledge-level in that it requires student recall, this item presents a problem and has one answer blank placed at the end.

Matching Exercises

As mentioned, a primary strength of the matching exercise is its effectiveness in measuring knowledge concerning associations of facts. There are instances, however, when it can also be a useful tool for measuring (a) understanding of general ideas (Comprehension) and (b) the ability to categorize and determine cause-and-effect relationships, understand the relationships among the parts of a unified whole, and understand metaphor (Analysis).

Mathematics

Knowledge Level: Students can recognize and recall previously learned information; no comprehension or understanding of the information is implied.

Memorization of formulae is necessary before mastering many computations. You can use the matching exercise as a means of determining your students' knowledge of these formulae.

On the line to the left of each geometric shape in Column A, write the corresponding letter of the formula for its area, from Column B. No formula may be used more than once.

	A		B
e	1. Circle	a.	A^2
f	2. Parallelogram	b.	AB
b	3. Rectangle	c.	BH
a	4. Square	d.	$\frac{1}{2} H (B_1 + B_2)$
d	5. Trapezoid	e.	πr^2
g	6. Triangle	f.	$\pi r^1 r^2$
		g.	$\frac{1}{2} BH$

Knowledge-level in that it tests students' recognition of memorized formulae, this exercise contains more possible responses than premises, and the directions specify that no response may be used more than once.

Comprehension Level: Students are able to understand or summarize information, translate information from one form or level to another, and comprehend data trends.

As part of a statistics unit, you may want to test your students' understanding of the appropriate application of formulae to given problems. This would not involve the actual application of these formulae (application), but it goes beyond the simple memorization of the formulae; instead, it calls for an understanding of which problems are appropriate for the application of specific formulae. The matching exercise is an efficient means for measuring such understanding.

In the blank next to each of the problems presented in Column A, write the letter of the statistical technique from Column B that should be used in its solution. No statistical technique may be used more than once.

	A		B
_b_	1. To estimate "heads" according to gender in 100 coin tosses	a.	Analysis of variance
_g_	2. Likely score obtained by guessing on a 100-item multiple-choice test	b.	Chi square
_c_	3. The effect a new spelling method had on one group of students	c.	Dependent *t*-test
_d_	4. Better of two reading methods on two groups of students	d.	Independent *t*-test
_a_	5. Most effective of three science methodologies on three groups of students	e.	Kuder-Richards-20
_e_	6. Comparing correct answers on odd versus even items on a true–false test	f.	Pearson *r*
_f_	7. Comparing two alternate forms of a test on the same group of students	g.	Probability formula
		h.	Standard deviation

This is a Comprehension-level exercise because it requires an understanding of the appropriateness of the formulae for particular situations. It has more possible responses than premises, and the directions specify that no technique may be used more than once.

Analysis Level: Students are able to break a unified whole into its basic parts and understand the relationship among those parts, compare and contrast phenomena, understand metaphors and analogies, understand the relationship between cause and effect, and categorize phenomena.

The ability to understand the relationships among the parts of a whole is a component of the Analysis level. For instance, you can use a matching item to sample your students' comprehension of the interrelationships among the parts of an algebraic equation.

In the blank to the left of each of the incomplete equations in Column A, write the letter of the missing part of the equation from Column B. No item from Column B may be used more than once.

	A		B
_c_ 1.	$(x + 6)\,(\underline{\quad}) = x^2 + 2x - 24$	a.	$(x - 7)$
_d_ 2.	$(x - 2)\,(\underline{\quad}) = x^2 + 5x - 14$	b.	$(x^2 + 6)$
_f_ 3.	$(x^2 + 3)\,(\underline{\quad}) = x^3 + 2x^2 + 3x + 6$	c.	$(x - 4)$
_e_ 4.	$(x^2 - 1)\,(\underline{\quad}) = x^4 - 1$	d.	$(x + 7)$
_b_ 5.	$(x^2 + 5)\,(\underline{\quad}) = x^4 + 11x^2 + 3$	e.	$(x^2 - 11)$
		f.	$(x + 2)$

This Analysis-level exercise requires students to understand how the parts of each equation relate to each other. There are more possible responses than premises, and the directions instruct that no possible response may be used more than once.

Science

Knowledge Level: Students can recognize and recall previously learned information; no comprehension or understanding of the information is implied.

Knowing the symbols of the chemical elements is essential for accomplishment of many of the activities that occur later. The matching exercise is an economical way of determining your students' knowledge of chemical elements and their symbols.

Beside each of the chemical elements in Column A, write the letter of the corresponding symbol from Column B. No symbol may be used more than once.

	A		B
_d_ 1.	Helium	a.	Fe
_f_ 2.	Hydrogen	b.	Na
_a_ 3.	Iron	c.	K
_h_ 4.	Neon	d.	He
_c_ 5.	Potassium	e.	Ti
_b_ 6.	Sodium	f.	H
_e_ 7.	Titanium	g.	Ni
		h.	Ne

A Knowledge-level exercise involving memory, its number of responses is greater than the number of premises, and the directions instruct that no symbol may be used more than once.

Comprehension Level: Students are able to understand or summarize information, translate information from one form or level to another, and comprehend data trends.

Understanding which formula to use in the solution of a specific scientific situation is a Comprehension-level performance. You can use a matching exercise like the following for sampling your students' comprehension of the appropriate formulae to use in the eventual solution of scientific problems.

> In the blank to the left of each of the problems in Column A, write the letter of the formula from Column B that should be used in its solution. No formula may be used more than once.

A	B
e 1. The force with which a falling glass hits the floor	a. $v = rt$
a 2. How fast a rabbit can run	b. $PV = nRT$
b 3. How much helium is needed to fill a balloon	c. $A = S^2$
f 4. Preparing a sucrose solution	d. $w = mg$
	e. $F = ma$
d 5. If I weigh 45 kg on the moon, what's my weight on earth?	f. $mv = m_2 v_2$

This Comprehension-level exercise requires students to match each of five problems with the formula appropriate for its solution. No memorization of the formulae is required (Knowledge), and no actual computations are required (Application); only an understanding of the appropriateness of formulae to problems is required (Comprehension). There are more formulae than problems, and the directions instruct that no formula may be used more than once.

Analysis Level: Students are able to break a unified whole into its basic parts and understand the relationship among those parts, compare and contrast phenomena, understand metaphors and analogies, understand the relationship between cause and effect, and categorize phenomena.

Determining cause–effect relationships is an Analysis-level process. To sample your students' ability to determine the results of weather phenomena, you can use the matching exercise.

Match each of the weather phenomena in Column A with its most likely effect from Column B. No effect from Column B may be used more than once.

A	B
_e_ 1. Acid rain	a. Debris
_d_ 2. Lightning	b. Floods
_b_ 4. Rain	c. Beautiful day
_a_ 3. Tornado	d. Fire
_f_ 5. Volcano	e. Ruined car paint
	f. Melted rocks

This Analysis-level exercise requires students to determine cause–effect relationships. Also, there are more results than causes, and the directions make clear that no result may be used more than once.

Social Studies

Knowledge Level: Students can recognize and recall previously learned information; no comprehension or understanding of the information is implied.

Knowing the respective capitals of the different states is essential to many geography lessons. You can use the matching exercise as an efficient means for measuring your students' memory of such associations.

On the line to the left of each of the states in Column A, write the letter of the name of its capital from Column B. No capital may be used more than once.

A	B
_h_ 1. California	a. Albany
_f_ 2. Louisiana	b. Austin
_g_ 3. Nevada	c. Dallas
_a_ 4. New York	d. Los Angeles
_b_ 5. Texas	e. New York City
	f. Baton Rouge
	g. Carson City
	h. Sacramento

The directions for this memory exercise instruct that none of the responses may be used more than once, although there are more response options than premises. These extra response options increase the probability that the correct responses will be chosen through direct selection rather than the process of elimination.

Comprehension Level: Students are able to understand or summarize information, translate information from one form or level to another, and comprehend data trends.

In many instances, positions in some organizations have counterparts in other organizations. This is a Comprehension-level concept because students must see that such positions are likely to have different names. You can use the matching exercise to sample your students' understanding of this concept.

On the lines beside each of the educational positions in Column A, write the letter of the corresponding federal government position from Column B. No federal government position may be used more than once.

A	B
_c_ 1. Superintendent	a. Attorney General
_d_ 2. Assistant Superintendent	b. Chief of Staff
_a_ 3. Solicitor	c. President
_e_ 4. Curriculum Director	d. Vice President
_f_ 5. Teacher	e. Senator
	f. Congressman

This matching exercise calls on students to understand that each of the educational positions has a single governmental counterpart, as specified in the directions; the governmental positions outnumber the educational positions, to reduce opportunities for guessing.

Analysis Level: Students are able to break a unified whole into its basic parts and understand the relationship among those parts, compare and contrast phenomena, understand metaphors and analogies, understand the relationship between cause and effect, and categorize phenomena.

To determine the extent to which your students can equate events with time periods, the matching exercise is an efficient tool. This does *not* involve the memorization of dates or events, which would be a Knowledge-level process, but rather the association of cause–effect relationships, an Analysis-level process.

In the blank next to each of the events in Column A, write the letter of its result from Column B. No result may be used more than once.

	A		B
c	1. Bombing of Pearl Harbor	a.	Start of U.S. Civil War
g	2. Bombing of Hiroshima	b.	End of U.S. Civil War
a	3. Firing on Fort Sumter	c.	Start of WWII
f	4. Firing at Lexington-Concord	d.	Start of WWI
d	5. Assassination of Archduke Ferdinand	e.	Start of War on Terrorism
		f.	Start of Revolutionary War
b	6. Signing at Appomattox Court House	g.	End of WWII

This exercise assesses students' ability to determine cause–effect relationships. Also, there are more effects than causes, and the directions specify that no effect may be used more than once.

English—Language Arts

Knowledge Level: Students can recognize and recall previously learned information; no comprehension or understanding of the information is implied.

Following a unit on American Literature, you may want to use the matching exercise as an economical means for determining your students' knowledge of literary works and their respective authors.

In the blank to the left of each literary work in Column A, write the letter of its author from Column B. *Authors may be used once, more than once, or not at all.*

A	B
_b_ 1. "Evangeline"	a. Oliver Wendell Holmes
_g_ 2. *Leaves of Grass*	b. Henry Wadsworth Longfellow
_d_ 3. *Life on the Mississippi*	c. Bret Harte
_d_ 4. *The Gilded Age*	d. Mark Twain
_c_ 5. "The Luck of Roaring Camp"	e. Harriet Beecher Stowe
_h_ 6. *The Red Badge of Courage*	f. John Greenleaf Whittier
_e_ 7. *Uncle Tom's Cabin*	g. Walt Whitman
	h. Stephen Crane

With its requirement for memorized associations, this is a Knowledge-level exercise. Structurally, the exercise is designed to prevent chance success in that the choices may be used once, more than once, or not at all, as specified in **bold italic type** in the directions.

Comprehension Level: Students are able to understand or summarize information, translate information from one form or level to another, and comprehend data trends.

Understanding that words have synonyms is an example of translating information from one form to another. You can use the matching exercise to sample your students' understanding of synonyms.

On the line to the left of each of the words in Column A, write the letter of its synonym from Column B. No synonym may be used more than once.

A	B
_h_ 1. Appreciative	a. Swift
_d_ 2. Blunt	b. Sharp
_e_ 3. Cold	c. Slothful
_a_ 4. Fast	d. Direct
_f_ 5. Hot	e. Frigid
_c_ 6. Lazy	f. Torrid
_g_ 7. Smart	g. Intelligent
	h. Grateful

Requiring students to see a different form of each word is a Comprehension-level activity. There are more possible responses than premises, and the directions state that no synonym may be used more than once.

Analysis Level: Students are able to break a unified whole into its basic parts and understand the relationship among those parts, compare and contrast phenomena, understand metaphors and analogies, understand the relationship between cause and effect, and categorize phenomena.

Since the ability to decipher metaphors is an Analysis-level process, you could use the matching exercise as a vehicle for checking on your students' ability to unravel given metaphors.

In the blank beside each of the metaphors in Column A, write the letter from Column B of the adjective that fits it. No adjective may be used more than once.

A	B
e 1. He is a fox	a. Ambitious
b 2. He is a worm	b. Cowardly
c 3. She is a deer	c. Fast
h 4. He is a bulldog	d. Gentle
i 5. She is a gold mine	e. Crafty
g 6. He is a weasel	f. Lazy
f 7. He is a sloth	g. Sneaky
d 8. She is a lamb	h. Tenacious
	i. Valuable

Analysis-level in that it requires the students to determine the adjectives that match metaphoric descriptions, this exercise has more adjectives than metaphors, and the directions instruct that no adjective may be used more than once.

SUMMARY

This chapter has covered three types of assessment items: true–false, completion or fill-in-the-blank, and matching. The true–false and completion items are best used for measurement in the lower cognitive levels as defined by Bloom's Taxonomy. The matching exercise is conducive to Analysis-level measurement in addition to its suitability for measurement in the two lower levels.

True–False Items

True–false items provide for wide sampling of Knowledge- and Comprehension-level performance in a comparatively short time period. We feel true–false items that go beyond these first two levels are confusing to students, thus preventing maximum performance. These items should be short, for ease of reading and understanding, and contain a single, noncontradictable statement. True–false items are an effective measurement tool within the major content areas.

Completion or Fill-In-the-Blank Items

Not to be confused with the short-answer item, the completion or fill-in-the-blank item is excellent for assessing the acquisition of factual information. Regrettably, however, this item is often poorly structured, to the confusion of student, or its wording provides unintentional clues to the correct response. However, with uniform structure and direct wording devoid of clues or insinuations, you can construct items that will neither confuse nor assist your students. This item is an effective measurement tool in all of the major content areas.

Matching Exercises

The matching exercise allows for a wide sampling of associative information within a relatively short period of time. This assessment tool is not confined to the Knowledge level; it can also effectively test students at the Comprehension and Analysis levels in all the major content areas. Yet valid assessment is dependent on clarity and specificity. Thus the wording and format should be understandable to students, but neither the wording nor the format should serve as clues to correct responses.

PROFESSIONAL DEVELOPMENT ACTIVITIES

1. In three- or four-member groups by content area, write a true–false item that samples student behavior at both the Knowledge and Comprehension levels. Be sure to review the guidelines for constructing

true–false items as well as the definitions of these two levels. Along with members from the other groups, put your Knowledge-level item on the board for discussion. Then do the same for your Comprehension-level item.

2. In your groups, write a Knowledge-level completion item. Review the guidelines carefully, remembering that the stem should present a problem to be answered in a *single* answer blank that will complete the sentence. Also, provide for one correct answer, but give no clues in the stem. Upon completion, put your item on the board for discussion, along with the items of the other groups.

3. In your groups, write one matching exercise for each of the following levels:

1. Knowledge

2. Comprehension

3. Analysis

Review your definitions for each of these cognitive levels and review the guidelines for constructing the matching exercise. You can use the chapter examples that pertain to your subject area as templates.

WWW RESOURCES

http://captain.park.edu/facultydevelopment/true–false.htm
This Web site of Park College furnishes information regarding the construction, strengths, and weaknesses of the true–false item.

http://web.utk.edu/~mccay/apdm/t_false/t-f_b.htm
This Web site of the Alabama Department of Education gives suggestions on the writing of matching, true–false, and completion questions.

http://www.edtech.vt.edu/edtech/id/assess/items.html
This Web site of The Virginia Polytechnic Institute presents pros and cons for various objective test items, including true–false and matching.

http://artswork.asu.edu/arts/teachers/assessment/forced2.htm
This Web site of Arizona State University gives suggestions on writing true–false questions.

4

Writing Multiple-Choice Items

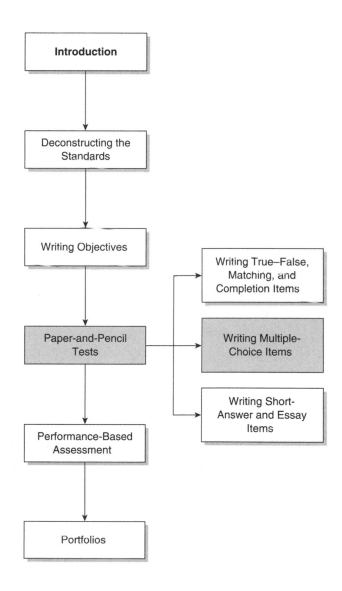

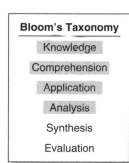

Bloom's Taxonomy
Knowledge
Comprehension
Application
Analysis
Synthesis
Evaluation

Introduction

Deconstructing the
Standards

Writing Objectives

Writing True–False,
Matching, and
Completion Items

Paper-and-Pencil
Tests

Writing Multiple-
Choice Items

Writing Short-
Answer and Essay
Items

Performance-Based
Assessment

Portfolios

With the nationwide dictate for standardized testing, your mandated involvement with multiple-choice items has probably already exceeded your projective powers and will likely persist indefinitely. Understandably, you may be as overwhelmed by these items as are your students. However, as this chapter demonstrates, there is reason for the widespread use of multiple-choice items on standardized as well as teacher-made tests.

As evidenced by the disproportionate number of psychometrically approved multiple-choice items on standardized achievement and aptitude tests, this may be the single most powerful, versatile, and economical test that is currently available to teachers, administrators, accountability officers, and admission officials. This does not indicate that this is the best test, however, because there is no such instrument. The best test is the one that best suits the examiner's purpose. Still, the multiple-choice test is readily adaptable to the measurement of academic achievement at most cognitive levels within each of the major content areas. It is conducive to the use of illustrations and interpretations and can measure the understanding and application of facts and concepts, as well as the ability to separate unified wholes into connected relationships. Moreover, it provides for a wide sampling of material during a relatively brief period of time at each of the hierarchical levels, with the exception of Synthesis and Evaluation, which we perceive as the only two levels within the Taxonomy that call for *divergent* as opposed to *convergent* thinking. To clarify, convergent thinking leads to conventionally accepted test answers, such as 2 + 2 = 4. Divergent thinking, on the other hand, can travel in many different directions, such as writing a unique story or defending a political position. We discuss the best options for testing divergent thinking in subsequent chapters.

A primary reason for the multiple-choice item's effectiveness in the measurement of higher-order thinking skills is its provision for homogeneous options: the more homogeneous the options, the more challenging the item. This homogeneity gives the multiple-choice test its discriminative powers.

A criticism of this item is the difficulty of devising a single best option. As previously mentioned, homogeneity within the options of an item is essential, but there has to be one best option. It is the responsibility of the test constructor to provide for one best response while simultaneously maintaining similarity among the distracters. Another problem is the difficulty in constructing plausible distracters. If two of the distracters on a four-option item are obviously incorrect, it becomes a true–false rather than a multiple-choice item. Yet such weakness can be avoided by competent and conscientious teachers.

GUIDELINES FOR CONSTRUCTION

For the test to be effective, it is important that students understand it. Otherwise, the teacher has no idea whether erring students simply do not know the answer or are confused by item wording or test format.

The stem of the multiple-choice item should vividly and succinctly present a problem that is answered by the correct option. The item can be presented as an incomplete sentence or simply as a question.

Incomplete Sentence

_____ The year Columbus first came to the New World was

A. 1865.

B. 1861.

C. 1776.

D. 1492.

Question

_____ In what year did Columbus first come to the New World?

A. 1865

B. 1861

C. 1776

D. 1492

The incomplete sentence is often preferred, but we suggest you use it only if it can be stated clearly and understandably. Rather than risk an awkward statement, which can involve time-consuming and questionable interpretation, state the item in question form. In either case, the item should usually be stated positively. When a negatively stated stem is preferred, the negative word (e.g., *not*) should be underlined or in *italics* so that the intent of the stem is clear.

_____ Which of the following is *not* a southern state?

A. Alabama

B. New York

C. Mississippi

D. Louisiana

Format the options vertically rather than horizontally for ease of isolation and comparison. As an additional deterrent to pupil confusion, make the options proportionately shorter than the stem, which also eases the comparison between possible solutions and the problem.

Teachers often wonder about the optimal number of options. Though there is a range of three to six options, having four or five seems to be the norm. Yet whether you prefer four or five options, you should be completely consistent throughout the test, thus providing a uniformity of structure that promotes concentration by eliminating the uneasiness that often accompanies uncertainty.

As we have stressed, students should not miss an item because of awkward wording or confusing format. They also should not make the correct response because of unintentional clues given by the test constructor, such as the patterning or consistent placement of correct responses. It does not take observant students long to discover an ACBD pattern or to see that the third option is most often the correct response. Such patterns and consistencies are understandable when you recognize the habitual nature of people (notice how students usually sit in the same classroom seats, even when seats are not assigned). The roll of a single die will ensure that your correct answers are randomly placed.

To make certain that there is one best answer, less-competent test constructors often make the correct option considerably longer or noticeably shorter than the distracters. In either case, the students may well select the correct option not because they know the answer but because they recognize unintentional clues.

Another attempt to provide for a best response is the inclusion of the "All of the above" option. Although this is acceptable, it should not always serve as the correct response; sometimes it should be a distracter. "None of the above" is another favorite option of neophyte test makers. A primary reason for its favored status is that neophyte teachers have exhausted their supply of plausible distracters. Since many students understand this, the item now has three, rather than four options.

CONTENT AREAS AND COGNITIVE LEVELS

As in Chapters 2 and 3, for each cognitive level in each content area, we start with a brief statement of the defining characteristics of that level.

Mathematics

Although not often used in this area, you can include multiple-choice items in your tests of mathematics achievement with assurance; they can effectively measure student performance at the Knowledge through the Analysis levels.

Knowledge Level: Students can recognize and recall previously learned information; no comprehension or understanding of the information is implied.

Since formulae are the foundation for solving a major proportion of mathematical problems, you can use the multiple-choice test to measure the extent to which your students have memorized specific formulae. Here is a sample test item:

   b The formula for determining the area of a triangle is

a. πr^2.

b. 1/2 bh.

c. lw.

d. (lw) $(\pi r^2)/2$.

This is a Knowledge-level item because it involves memorization. It is structurally sound in that the stem is long, the options are short and the same length, the distracters are plausible, and it provides for one correct answer.

Comprehension Level: Students are able to understand or summarize information, translate information from one form or level to another, and comprehend data trends.

Translating information from one form or level to another is a Comprehension-level activity, and you can use the multiple-choice item to determine if your students understand that fractions and decimals are representations of the same value, as in the following example.

   c The decimal equivalent of ¾ is

a. 0.35

b. 0.65

c. 0.75

d. 0.85

In this Comprehension-level item, students must translate information from one form to another. The stem is straightforward, devoid of ambiguities, and the options are brief and plausible, with only one correct answer.

Application Level: Students are able to take information that has previously been acquired and comprehended and use it in concrete situations.

Many statistical computations take place at the Application level. After introducing central tendency (mean, median, mode), wide margins on test pages can allow your students to compute the arithmetic mean, as in the following example.

_a_ What is the arithmetic mean of 35, 45, 55, 60?

a. 48.75

b. 50.75

c. 52.75

d. 54.75

This item is Application-level because finding the correct response necessitates applying a formula. Although it requires a computational process, the brevity of the problem allows for the computations on the test copy itself. Also, the options are brief, with plausible distracters and one correct answer.

Analysis Level: Students are able to break a unified whole into its basic parts and understand the relationship among those parts, compare and contrast phenomena, understand metaphors and analogies, understand the relationship between cause and effect, and categorize phenomena.

The Venn Diagram is an excellent vehicle for acquainting students with numerical relationships, an Analysis-level activity. To measure how well your students have learned this information and how well you have taught it, you can use multiple-choice items, such as the one that follows.

_a_ In a junior class of 320 students, 85 are taking chemistry, 200 are taking American Literature, and 60 are taking both. How many are taking chemistry or American Literature?

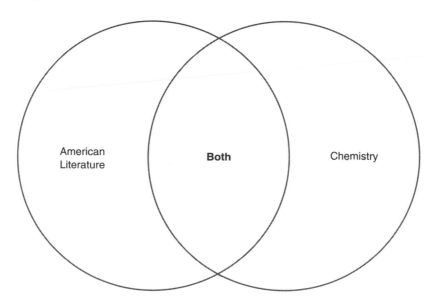

a. 225

b. 320

c. 165

d. 60

This Analysis-level item requires students to examine the relationships among the number of students enrolled in one of two courses or in both. Its stem contains no extraneous material, all options are brief, the distracters are believable, and there is only one correct answer.

Science

The natural sciences lend themselves well to both performance-based and paper-and-pencil assessment, and we advocate a combination of the two. Paper-and-pencil assessments do not allow for the in-depth scrutiny provided by performance-based assessments, but they can cover broad latitudes of material. The multiple-choice test allows for effective assessment of the Knowledge through the Analysis levels.

Knowledge Level: Students can recognize and recall previously learned information; no comprehension or understanding of the information is implied.

Knowing the Periodic Table is a prerequisite of most lab experiments in chemistry classes. Rather than have students reproduce the entire chart, you can sample their knowledge of the chemical symbols with multiple-choice items like the following:

___a___ The chemical symbol for lead is

a. Pb

b. Au

c. Fe

d. Cu

Requiring rote memorization, this item has a proportionately long stem, along with short options containing plausible distracters and one correct answer.

Comprehension Level: Students are able to understand or summarize information, translate information from one form or level to another, and comprehend data trends.

Understanding what one has seen or witnessed is a Comprehension-level achievement. If you have conducted a classroom demonstration and wish to learn how well your students have comprehended what you did, you can use a multiple-choice item like the following:

_b_ Which of the following did *not* occur in yesterday's lab demonstration?

a. Soda was mixed with vinegar.

b. The mixture was stirred.

c. The teacher wore gloves.

d. The solution erupted.

This Comprehension-level item tests whether students understood or comprehended the lab demonstration. The stem is proportionately long but devoid of ambiguities, the word *not* is in bold type so as to avoid confusion, and the options are short and plausible with one correct answer.

Application Level: Students are able to take information that has been acquired and comprehended and use it in a concrete situation.

Virtually every time your students use a formula to solve a problem, real or hypothetical, they are operating at the Application level. Having acquainted your chemistry students with the Periodic Table at the Knowledge level, you can see if they can use it in the solution of a problem by using a multiple-choice item like the following.

_d_ The atomic mass of H_2O is

a. 12.

b. 14.

c. 16.

d. 18.

The correct answer to this item is dependent on students' application of the Periodic Table. Its stem is succinct and understandable, and the options are terse, with believable distracters and a single correct answer.

Analysis Level: Students are able to break a unified whole into its basic parts and understand the relationship among those parts, compare and contrast phenomena, understand metaphors and analogies, understand the relationship between cause and effect, and categorize phenomena.

In order to make distinctions between phenomena, we compare and contrast them. You can use the multiple-choice test to determine the extent to which your students can compare, contrast, and make fine discriminations between rock types, for instance. Here is a sample item:

_c_ The greatest similarity between an igneous rock and a metamorphic rock is their

a. foliation.

b. fossilization.

c. composition.

d. texture.

In this analytic comparison, students must use their discriminative abilities to determine the most significant similarity between the two rock types. The stem of the item specifies what the students are to determine, and although the options are brief and homogenous, there is only one best answer.

Social Studies

As much as with any other content area, the Knowledge level is prerequisite to higher-order activities in the social studies area. Since much basic information is necessary before your students are able to comprehend, apply, and analyze it, you need to know how much of this basic information they have acquired. The multiple-choice test is an excellent tool because it provides for wide, economical sampling regarding time and space.

Knowledge Level: Students can recognize and recall previously learned information; no comprehension or understanding of the information is implied.

Secondary social studies teachers know the importance of students' awareness of the capital cities of the various states. A quick and simple means for revealing their awareness is a multiple-choice item like the following.

_c_ The capital of Nevada is

a. Reno.

b. Las Vegas.

c. Carson City.

d. Tahoe.

A Knowledge-level item requiring simple recognition, the item has a clear but terse structure and provides for a single best answer among three plausible distracters.

Comprehension Level: Students are able to understand or summarize information, translate information from one form or level to another, and comprehend data trends.

Understanding that the same data can be depicted in a variety of ways is Comprehension-level behavior. If your students have been displaying data on charts and graphs, you can see if they understand that the same data can be reflected within a multiplicity of both charts and graphs by constructing a multiple-choice item like the following:

_a_ Which of the following charts or graphs displays the same information as the histogram shown above?

a. Bar graph

b. Pie chart

c. Line graph

d. Picture chart

This Comprehension-level item requires students to see the same information displayed by two different media, and structurally, the item has a proportionately long stem followed by brief options containing plausible distracters and a single correct answer.

Application Level: Students are able to take information that has been acquired and comprehended and use it in a concrete situation.

As students progress from elementary to secondary school, so do their skills. As you guide your students in increasing their map skills, you can ask them to go from Point A to Point B via Points C and D, instead of just asking them to compute the distance from Point A to B. To sample how well they can do this, you can use the following type of multiple-choice item.

_b_ According to the map shown, the distance from Port Arthur to College Station, via Liberty and Conroe, is

a. 175 miles.

b. 180 miles.

c. 185 miles.

d. 190 miles.

In this Application item, students must engage in a more complex process to compute the distance of a sequential rather than a direct route. The stem instructs them in precisely what is expected of them. Also, the distracters are terse and believable, and there is only one correct answer.

Analysis Level: Students are able to break a unified whole into its basic parts and understand the relationship among those parts, compare and contrast phenomena, understand metaphors and analogies, understand the relationship between cause and effect, and categorize phenomena.

Determining cause–effect relationships requires complex thought processes, and prioritizing such relationships is even more difficult. Let's say your secondary social studies students have been investigating the causes for conflict between nations. To sample the extent of their ability to scrutinize such causes, you can construct multiple-choice items such as the following:

   b   The primary reason for the Hamas terrorists' hatred of the United States is the U.S.'s

   a. democratic political system.

   b. friendship with Israel.

   c. involvement in the Persian Gulf War.

   d. historical involvement in slavery.

In this item, students must make fine discriminations in their analyses of cause–effect relationships, as set forth in the stem of the item. Structurally, the options are comparatively brief, there is one best answer, and the distracters are believable.

English–Language Arts

The versatility of the multiple-choice item is highly visible in the measurement of student achievement within this content area. It is appropriate for use in the Knowledge, Comprehension, Application, and Analysis levels. Its range includes the knowledge of vocabulary definitions, an understanding of the settings of literary works, the application of grammar and punctuation skills, the perception of symbolic usage, and comparisons between literary works. Moreover, it allows for measurement of these components with economy of time and space.

Knowledge Level: Students can recognize and recall previously learned information; no comprehension or understanding of the information is implied.

If your students are going to become acquainted with the literary works of any period, they must first know who wrote them. Let's say you have begun a unit on Early American Literature. As a formative assessment, you can find out what your students know about the basics of this period using items like the following.

___c___ The author of *Poor Richard's Almanac* is

a. Thomas Jefferson.

b. George Washington.

c. Benjamin Franklin.

d. Samuel Adams.

This Knowledge-level item, involving rote memorization, has a clear and precise stem and short options, with three plausible distracters and one best answer.

Comprehension Level: Students are able to understand or summarize information, translate information from one form or level to another, and comprehend data trends.

When you give your secondary English students a spelling test and have them write the definitions of the words, they are performing at the Knowledge level. To elevate them to the Comprehension level, where one of the requirements is to transfer information from one form to another, you can see if your students comprehend synonyms. Multiple-choice items like the following sample your students' ability in this area.

___d___ A synonym for *celebrate* is

a. shout.

b. shriek.

c. laugh.

d. rejoice.

By correctly responding, students have demonstrated their comprehension of the shared meaning of the two words: they can see that the word can be translated to another form. Structurally, the item has a proportionately long stem with no excessive material, three short and plausible distracters, and a single but brief best answer.

Application Level: Students are able to take information that has been acquired and comprehended and use it in a concrete situation.

Correct punctuation is defined by specific rules. Having acquainted your secondary English students with these rules and their usages, you could use items like the following sample to assess their ability to apply those rules.

___d___ What is the correct ending punctuation for the following sentence? "Quickly, the wall has collapsed"

a. .

b. ?

c. :

d. !

This Application-level item calls for students to use punctuation skills, which they have acquired and comprehended, in a new situation. The stem defines a problem to be answered by one of the brief options, placed among three plausible distracters.

Analysis Level: Students are able to break a unified whole into its basic parts and understand the relationship among those parts, compare and contrast phenomena, understand metaphors and analogies, understand the relationship between cause and effect, and categorize phenomena.

Unraveling literary symbolism can be a challenging Analysis-level undertaking. As your secondary English students move into the classics, they will encounter many forms of symbolism. The following multiple-choice item could help you determine whether your students can decipher a symbolic meaning from William Faulkner's "A Rose for Emily."

___a___ In Faulkner's short story, "A Rose for Emily," Emily represents

a. the Old South.

b. women's suffrage.

c. the Civil Rights Movement.

d. Scarlett O'Hara.

Since it requires students to unravel the meaning of a symbolic literary personality, this is an Analysis-level item. Its stem is proportionately long but devoid of excessive information, and the options are short, with plausible distracters and one correct answer.

SUMMARY

The multiple-choice test is powerful and versatile, providing for wide coverage in a relatively short period of time and allowing for measurement of both basic and higher-order thinking processes. However, poorly constructed items can negate these strengths. The multiple-choice item is easily adaptable to any content area in the middle and secondary schools and it also provides for measurement at the Knowledge, Comprehension, Application, and Analysis levels.

PROFESSIONAL DEVELOPMENT ACTIVITIES

First, assemble into three-or four-member groups by subject area. Once assembled, each group is to construct two or three multiple-choice items within each of the following levels: Knowledge, Comprehension, Application, and Analysis, after reviewing the "Guidelines for Construction" section of this chapter and the definitions of the four cognitive levels.

When you have finished constructing your items, one representative from each group is to put a Knowledge-level item on the board for discussion and constructive criticism. After these multiple-choice items have been scrutinized, other groups can follow until there is consensus to move on to Comprehension. Continue these procedures through the Analysis level.

As you observe the items on the board, first determine whether each item is actually measuring the intended cognitive level by reexamining the definitions of the four levels. Next, check whether the items are constructed in compliance with the suggested guidelines.

WWW RESOURCES

http://artswork.asu.edu/arts/teachers/assessment/forced1.htm
This Web site of the Arizona State University and the Arizona Board of Regents provides suggestions regarding the strengths, weaknesses, and construction of multiple-choice items.

http://www.edtech.vt.edu/edtech/id/assess/items.html
This Web site of The Virginia Polytechnic Institute presents pros and cons of the multiple-choice item, as well as suggestions for its construction.

http://www.tenet.edu/teks/science/assessment/methods/selected.html
This Web site of the University of Texas, Austin, offers suggestions regarding the strengths, weaknesses, uses, and construction of multiple-choice items.

http://www.wmich.edu/grad/gatraining/TAgetting1.htm
This Web site of Western Michigan University provides suggestions for the construction of multiple-choice items.

5 Writing Short-Answer and Essay Items

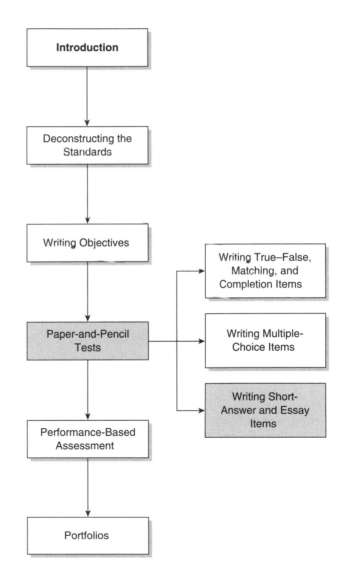

INTRODUCTION

The Short-Answer Item

Some measurement specialists equate the **short-answer** with the completion item, perceiving its usefulness as confined to the Knowledge level. Others see no difference between the short-answer and the completion items in either usefulness or structure. As we demonstrate, however, the horizontal versatility of the short-answer item transcends the major content areas, and it is adaptable to every level in the cognitive domain. Since many state assessment tests contain open-ended questions, skill in responding to short-answer items can improve your students' scores on these high-stakes tests.

Structure

As we mention in Chapter 3, the completion item is an incomplete sentence with a single blank at the end of the item. The short-answer item, however, is structured as either a question or a command:

Question: What is the sum of 38 + 24?

Command: Solve the problem 38 + 24.

As with the completion item, neither the question nor command form of the short-answer item should provide for multiple answers.

Bad: When did Columbus first come to the New World?

Answer: When Queen Isabella financed his voyage (or, In 1492).

Good: In what year did Columbus first come to the New World?

Answer: 1492

The short-answer item also should be structured to avoid unintentional clues:

Bad: List the three primary colors.

Good: List each of the primary colors.

(The term *each* indicates that all of the primary colors are to be listed, but it does not specify the number of primary colors, thus avoiding an unintentional clue.)

The Essay Item

The **essay item**, in our opinion, is one of the most misunderstood, misused, and abused items within the entire paper-and-pencil domain. It has definite strengths, but it is also prone to pronounced weaknesses, some of which are attributable to the construction and scoring of the item. In this chapter, we show you how to avoid construction and scoring weaknesses.

A primary strength of the essay item is its provision for an in-depth, detailed analysis of a small area of material (Analysis level). This item further permits assessment of students' organizational, creative, and writing skills; their ability to build a case and make a point; and their capacity to evaluate phenomena, all of which occur at the Synthesis and Evaluation levels. Also, it is comparatively easy to construct. However, it is of limited use for assessing broad latitudes of content.

Scoring essay items requires expertise, especially since some students are adept at talking around a point. However, clearly defined items and adherence to corresponding **rubrics,** as we discuss later, will neutralize any diversionary tactics devised by an ill-informed student. Also problematic to the neophyte or inattentive teacher are secondary factors, such as spelling, handwriting, and neatness, but well-constructed rubrics can minimize or even negate such distractions: They can illuminate responses that do not meet specified criteria, regardless of how neat and verbally correct they may be.

As with the short-answer item, student skills in writing essay responses have become increasingly important with the implementation of open-ended questions on statewide examinations. When you know how to construct and score essay responses, aware of the strengths and weaknesses of these items as well which cognitive levels are most conducive to their assessment, the result will be higher student scores on both high-stakes state examinations and on your own tests.

Construction

Following an essay exam, a common answer to the question, "How did you do?" is, "I don't know . . . it depends on what the teacher wants." If this is the response, the items are probably vague, and if students do not understand the question, how can you determine whether they know the answer? Of course, the item should not contain clues to its answer, but it should specify exactly what is expected of the students, so it is important to structure the item to include the specific points that should appear in the students' responses. For example, the item may begin with a task-directed statement:

Within two pages, compare and contrast how George Washington and Francis Marion contributed to the Revolutionary War. In your narrative, cite one similarity and one difference, including two supporting arguments for each. Your essay should be well organized as well as grammatically and linguistically sound.

Beginning with a task-directed statement, this item leaves no doubt as to what is expected of the student.

Scoring

Rubrics should be used to score essay items. Rubrics in this context are scoring guides, delineating a point spread for each item and the bases for awarding the points (or a similar general explanation), including partial credit for partially right responses. In some instances, they are best developed as tests are constructed, although generic rubrics can also be helpful. In either case, they help ensure consistency, objectivity, and fairness in scoring, and we strongly advocate their use.

For instance, using the previous example, the cited similarity and difference could each have a zero to three-point value, depending on the selection and presentation. Then the four supporting arguments could have a zero- to three-point range, based on their relevancy and significance. Although the item stresses organizational, grammatical, and linguistic soundness, these skills should previously have been taught if they are to have rubric point value. If they have not been taught, they should not be factored into the rubric.

Generic rubrics are appropriate for multiple classroom situations. As Arter and McTighe (2001, p. 27) point out, they are "useful to help students understand the nature of quality—the 'big picture' details that contribute to the quality of a type of performance or product." They go on to explain that "task-specific scoring could happen in mathematics, social studies, science, and any class that has a particular content to be learned (p. 28)." In describing task-specific rubrics, they acknowledge that these rubrics "allow students to see what quality looks like in a simple problem— the one at hand" (p. 27). Such rubrics also provide for analytic scoring.

Although it is cumbersome, we recommend scoring essay tests item by item as opposed to paper by paper. This strategy assists you in focusing on a specific area, allowing you to detect patterns in student responses (e.g., a number of students omitting the same point), which may indicate the need to adjust your instruction or the item itself. The item-by-item method also allows you to score the papers more anonymously; you are assessing responses rather than students, thus negating the halo effect. For example, if Fred has previously performed well, you may assume that he is going to perform well on this particular assignment and thus award him undeserved points. Of course, with the scoring of any test—and especially the essay test—if you become tired, stressed, or hungry, stop immediately and do not resume until you have regained homeostasis.

SHORT-ANSWER ITEMS, CONTENT AREAS, AND COGNITIVE DOMAIN LEVELS

In the following examples, we demonstrate that the short-answer item is adaptable to each of the cognitive hierarchical levels within the major content areas. As in Chapters 2, 3 and 4, we start with a brief statement of the defining characteristics for each cognitive level in each content area.

Mathematics

Knowledge Level: Students can recognize and recall information; no comprehension or understanding of information is expected.

To sample your students' knowledge of formulae for computing the areas of geometrical figures, short-answer items are suitable. For example,

Write the formula for the area of an ellipse.

Answer: $r_1 r_2$

Testing student knowledge of a memorized formula, the item is in the form of a direct command that calls for a single answer.

Comprehension Level: Students are able to understand or summarize information, translate information from one form or level to another, and comprehend data trends.

As a means of sampling students' ability to translate mathematical information from one form to another, you can use the short-answer item.

If $x = 3$ and $y = 2$, $2x + 7y = 20$. Illustrate the commutative property by reversing the x and y *places*, but do *not* change the values of x and y. What is the sum? Show your work.

Answer: $7y + 2x = 20$

This is a Comprehension item because the equations in both the command and the student answer are forms of each other, each having a sum of 20. This item demonstrates that students can learn while arriving at the answer to the item, thus comprehending that the equation has another form. Moreover, the wording is clear, providing for one answer but furnishing no clues.

Application Level: Students are able to take information that has been acquired and comprehended and use it in concrete situations.

In a unit on area, you can use short-answer items to sample your students' skills in applying formulae to actual situations. For example,

> Jamal has a garden that is 12' × 8'. How much will fencing cost to enclose his garden if fencing costs $3.00 per foot? Show all of your work.

Perimeter = 2L + 2W

Answer:	12	8	24	$3.00
	×2	×2	+16	× 40
	24	16	40	$120.00 = Cost of fencing

This is an Application problem because the students must apply a formula to given dimensions and then multiply the total by a given cost per unit. The problem is clearly presented, devoid of excessive wording, and calls for one correct answer. However, it is your prerogative to award partial credit, as long as your decision is based on consistent criteria.

Analysis Level: Students are able to break a unified whole into its basic parts and understand the relationship among those parts, compare and contrast phenomena, understand metaphors and analogies, understand the relationship between cause and effect, and categorize phenomena.

A demonstrated understanding of analogies reflects Analysis-level competence, and you can use short-answer items to sample your students' ability in this area.

> If 5 is to 25 as 6 is to 36, create a number analogy for 7 and one for 9.
>
> Answer: 7 is to 49 as 9 is to 81.

This is an Analysis-level item in that the students must first understand the analogous relationship between the two pairs of numbers in the command; then, they must evidence their understanding by writing two prescribed analogies in the answer space. The item is clear and specific in its instruction and calls for definite answers without supplying clues to the answers. Nevertheless, you must establish the point value of the item beforehand and whether to award partial credit for incomplete answers.

Synthesis Level: Students are able to assemble parts into a new whole, formulate new hypotheses or plans of action, and construct solutions to unfamiliar problems. Many Synthesis-level processes involve divergent thinking, which is thinking that can travel in many different directions, with no predetermined single correct answer. This is not to imply that there are no item guidelines or that all student responses are acceptable. The item should clearly and succinctly specify what is expected of the student.

After your students have studied various geometrical shapes and some of their practical functions, you can use the short-answer item to sample their creative use of these shapes. For example,

> Draw a diagram of a building containing *three* geometrical shapes. Be sure to circle each of the shapes.
>
> Possible answer (see figure):

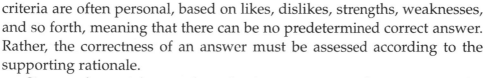

This is a Synthesis-level item in that it calls for the students to create diagrams of buildings containing geometrical shapes. Providing for divergent thinking, this item could have as many correct answers as there are students. It is your decision as whether to award partial credit. For example, a minimum of one point could be given for each figure and a maximum of three points for each shape, depending on creativity.

Evaluation Level: Students are able to make value judgments based on predetermined criteria or internal consistency. Remember that predetermined criteria are often personal, based on likes, dislikes, strengths, weaknesses, and so forth, meaning that there can be no predetermined correct answer. Rather, the correctness of an answer must be assessed according to the supporting rationale.

Since polynomials may be solved in a variety of ways, it can be advantageous to learn if and why individual students prefer one method over others. Short-answer items are an excellent source for uncovering the bases for these choices, as shown in the following example.

> The equation $(x^3 + y)(x^3 + y)$ can be solved in more than one way [e.g., $(x^3 + y)^2$, $x^6 + 2x^3y + y^2$, a programmed graphing calculator]. Select a method and list *three* reasons for your choice.

Possible answer: I would use my calculator because

1. it's faster.
2. I'm not very good at factoring.
3. I never learned the first method $(x^3 + y)^2$.

This Evaluation item calls on students to make value judgments based on particular criteria, in this instance, the students' appraisals of their relative strengths and weaknesses in solving polynomials. You can learn from the sample response that the student needs additional instruction in factoring and to be introduced to the Foil method. As a suggested rubric, there could be an allotted three points for each reason, depending on the rationale of each.

Science

Knowledge Level: Students can recall information; no comprehension or understanding of information is expected.

To sample your students' basic geological knowledge, short-answer items like the following can be effective.

List each of the Earth's layers.

Answer: Crust

Mantle

Outer Core

Inner Core

Requiring the recall of memorized material, this Knowledge-level item avoids any quantitative clues by using the term *each* as opposed to "four." In the form of a command, its directness eliminates irrelevant answers.

Comprehension Level: Students are able to understand or summarize information, translate information from one form or level to another, and comprehend data trends.

During a unit on the human body, you can determine the extent to which your students understand that some body parts have more than one name. The short-answer test is an excellent means for making such a determination.

What is another name for a blood cell?

Answer: Corpuscle

Comprehension-level in that it requires the transfer of a term (blood cell) from one form to another (corpuscle), this question-form short-answer item is clear, direct, provides for a correct answer, and furnishes no clues.

Application Level: Students are able to take information that has been acquired and comprehended and use it in concrete situations.

As a part of a unit on electricity, you can give your students problems centering on amperage, voltage, resistance, and wattage. Short-answer items are most adaptable to such opportunities.

If a wire has a resistance of 5 ohms and a traveling current of 12 amps, what is its voltage?

$V = IR$

Answer: $5 \times 12 = 60$ volts

This is an Application item in that students must apply a memorized formula in a concrete situation. Succinct and clearly stated, the item calls for a simple, correct answer and furnishes no clues.

Analysis Level: Students are able to break a unified whole into its basic parts and understand the relationship among those parts, compare and contrast phenomena, understand metaphors and analogies, understand the relationship between cause and effect, and categorize phenomena.

Virtually any type of investigation necessitates an analytic process. For instance, you can use a short-answer item to assess your students' ability to identify gestation periods on the basis of given clues.

Which rodent has a longer gestation period than the golden hamster but a shorter one than the rat?

Answer: Mouse

Analysis-level in that it requires arriving at the correct answer through an analysis of given clues, this item calls for a correct answer without providing unwarranted clues. If there could be an unanticipated correct answer, however, you must give credit for it.

Synthesis Level: Students are able to demonstrate the ability to assemble parts into a new whole, formulate new hypotheses or plans of action, and construct solutions to unfamiliar problems. Many Synthesis-level processes involve divergent thinking, which is thinking that can travel in many different directions. For items testing at this level, there can be no single correct answers. This does not indicate, however, that there are no guidelines or that all student responses are acceptable. Indeed, the item should clearly and succinctly specify what is expected of the students.

You can use the short-answer item to assess your students' creative skills in addressing environmental issues, for example, as in the following:

List *two* procedures that you would initiate to clean up a polluted pond in your town.

Possible answer: 1. Contact an environmental group for assistance.

2. Call the local newspaper.

Synthesis-level in that it calls for solutions to an unfamiliar problem, this item is clear, direct, and specific and provides for student creativity without supplying unwarranted clues. Although the item solicits divergent thinking, which proceeds in multiple directions and precludes a single, predetermined correct answer, you must still determine scoring criteria for the item and be consistently objective in your assessment of each student's response. For example, you could provide a maximum of four points for each procedure, depending on feasibility and originality.

Evaluation Level: Students are required to make value judgments based on predetermined criteria or internal consistency. It should be remembered that predetermined criteria are often personal, based on likes, dislikes, strengths, weaknesses, and so on. Hence, there can be no predetermined correct answer, and the correctness of an answer should be assessed according to the supporting rationale.

Whether to rebuild houses in a floodplain, an area that has a history of flooding, is controversial and often the focus of value judgments based on individuals' personal criteria. In such situations, it is wise to present the facts to the students and then allow them to derive their own ethical positions. Short-answer items can determine your students' positions on a given issue. It is important that you score the students according to the rationale for their respective positions rather than their positions per se.

Do you favor or oppose rebuilding houses in an area that has a history of being flooded? List two (2) reasons for your position.

Possible answer: I favor it because

1. Since a person's family has always lived there, it is meant to be that he lives there, too.

2. Since the cost of living there is low, people can afford to pay the flood insurance and live in an area they like, even if they have to rebuild.

This is an Evaluation item in that it asks for a value judgment without leading the students. However, regardless of whether you agree with students' positions, the first reason is rather weak because virtually anything can be construed as "it is meant to be." You should concentrate on students' rationales for their positions rather than on the position itself. As a suggested rubric, you could allot three points for each reason, on the basis of logic and rationale, and five points for overall consistency and continuity among the reasons.

Social Studies

Knowledge Level: Students can recall information; no comprehension or understanding of information is expected.

Following a unit on the Civil War, you can use the short-answer test to sample your students' knowledge of key figures in this great conflict.

What is the name of the town in which General Lee officially surrendered to General Grant?

Answer: Appomattox Court House

Knowledge-level involving simple recall, this command-form item is precise in its questioning.

Comprehension Level: Students are able to understand or summarize information, translate information from one form or level to another, and comprehend data trends.

Often, political and military events are known by more than one name. You could use the short-answer item as a motivational source for directing your students toward an understanding of this concept.

What is another official term for the Battle of Bull Run?

Answer: The Battle of Manassas

In responding to this question-form short answer, students are translating information from one form to another. Succinct and direct, the item uses the term *official* as a deterrent against inappropriate answers, thus providing for a correct answer without supplying unwarranted clues.

Application Level: Students are able to take information that has been acquired and comprehended and use it in concrete situations.

During a demographic unit, you can give your students the opportunity to use the gender ratio formula in a concrete situation, using a short-answer item like the following:

What was the Megabirth Hospital's January gender ratio if 475 girls and 400 boys were born? Carry your figure to one decimal place and show all of your work.

Answer: Gender ratio = (male/female) × 100

Gender ratio = (400 male/475 female) = 0.842 × 100 = 84.2

Requiring the application of memorized formula in a concrete situation, this is an Application-level item. Although the item is direct and specifically stated, it is left to you to determine beforehand whether partial points are awarded for answers that deviate from the precise 84.2.

Analysis Level: Students are able to break a unified whole into its basic parts and understand the relationship among those parts, compare and contrast phenomena, understand metaphors and analogies, understand the relationship between cause and effect, and categorize phenomena.

Determining the temporal relationship of events becomes an Analysis-level process when these events are presented in a scrambled order with some of the events excluded from the list. This is because arranging the events in chronological order necessitates comparing the events with each other (e.g., one event is third instead of second or fourth because of its relationship with the other events). You can use a short-answer item to determine your students' ability to arrange historical events in chronological order from a scrambled list, as in the following example:

Arrange these American wars in chronological order:

Vietnam War
Persian Gulf War
Revolutionary War
World War I
War of 1812
Spanish American War
Civil War
Korean War

Answer:

Revolutionary War
War of 1812
Civil War
Spanish American War
World War I
Korean War
Vietnam War
Persian Gulf War

With several American wars excluded from the list, arranging the wars in chronological order is an Analysis-level task because it requires the students to compare the time periods of the wars with each other. The item is clear, to the point, and requires a single answer without supplying any hints. You can decide whether to award partial credit if the wars are not listed in exact chronological order.

Synthesis Level: Students are able to assemble parts into a new whole, formulate new hypotheses or plans of action, and construct solutions to unfamiliar problems. Many Synthesis-level processes involve divergent thinking, which is thinking that can travel in many different directions, with no single correct answers. This is not to imply that there are no item guidelines, however, or that all student responses are acceptable. Indeed, the item should clearly and succinctly specify what is expected of the students.

More often than not, conflicts are resolved through compromises. You could assess your students' ability to use their creativity in devising compromises as solutions to international conflicts, for instance, through items like the following.

Within two sentences, propose a compromise for resolving the Israeli–Palestinian conflict.

Possible answer: The Israelis will refrain from any military action against the Palestinians for suicide bombings if the Palestinian authorities punish those who ordered the bombings.

This item necessitates a creative solution to a problem. Since it is a short-answer rather than an essay item, details are not required. Nevertheless, you should establish criteria upon which to score the item and consistently apply them to each student response. For instance, you could allot up to five points for the logic, originality, and potential success of the plan.

Evaluation Level: Students are required to make value judgments based on predetermined criteria or internal consistency. Remember that predetermined criteria are often personal, based on likes, dislikes, strengths, weaknesses, and so on and that there can be no predetermined correct answer. Rather, the correctness of an answer should be assessed according to the supporting rationale.

The issue of cutting trees in old-growth forests (trees at least 100 years old) is an impetus for the formation of value judgments. After objective examination of this issue in class, you can assess your students' judgment of the controversy through an item like the following:

List three (3) reasons explaining whether you favor or oppose cutting down trees in old-growth forests.

Possible answer: I favor it because

1. Trees are not people or animals.
2. Trees can stand in the way of progress.
3. Trees can be replaced.

Since it involves a value judgment, this is an Evaluation-level item, even though its structure restricts a detailed explanation justifying this sample student rationale. Regardless, the reasoning seems shallow, having omitted some of the major arguments supporting the cutting of trees (e.g., some of them may be dying). Hence, even if you agree with the student's position, you must score the rationale, not the position. The rubric could provide a maximum of three points for each supporting reason, based on logic and consistency.

English–Language Arts

Knowledge Level: Students can recall information; no comprehension or understanding of information is expected.

You can use the short-answer test to sample your students' knowledge of authors, as in this example:

Write the first, middle, and last birth name, not pen name, of the author of *Silas Marner.*

Answer: Mary Ann Evans

Knowledge-level, involving rote memorization, this item requires students to know *two* specific facts: (1) the pen name of an author and (2) the author's first, middle, and last birth name. Structurally, the item is clear and direct and provides for a single answer.

Comprehension Level: Students are able to understand or summarize information, translate information from one form or level to another, and comprehend data trends.

As a means of sampling your students' comprehension of textual content, you can use a short-answer item like the following:

> What type of natural geologic formation held a lost Tom Sawyer and Becky Thatcher?
>
> Answer: A cave

This item checks students' reading comprehension skills (as well as whether they have read the assignment). The term *natural formation* deters irrelevant answers (e.g., "house"), thus providing for a correct answer without supplying a clue.

Application Level: Students are able to take information that has been acquired and comprehended and use it in concrete situations.

Using an assigned word in a written sentence is an Application-level activity. You can use short-answer items to measure your students' ability in this capacity, as in this example:

> Use your vocabulary word *panegyrical* in an interrogative sentence. Do your best with respect to punctuation, grammar, capitalization, and spelling.
>
> Possible answer: Do you think your critique of the author is somewhat panegyrical?

With the caution for optimal use of mechanics, you have the option of whether to include the usage of general mechanics in the point value of the item. If you decide to do so, you must determine the quantitative value of each.

Analysis Level: Students are able to break a unified whole into its basic parts and understand the relationship among those parts, compare and contrast phenomena, understand metaphors and analogies, understand the relationship between cause and effect, and categorize phenomena.

Deciphering the meaning of literary symbolism is an analytic endeavor. You can use short-answer items such as the following to sample your students' ability to detect symbolic meaning in their literature assignments.

What do the Salem witch trials symbolize in *The Crucible?*

Answer: The McCarthy hearings.

This is an Analysis-level item because the students must unravel many subtleties within the story to determine the answer. The students' phrasing may differ somewhat, but the answer to this succinct and direct question does not change, despite the absence of any clues.

Synthesis Level: Students are able to assemble parts into a new whole, formulate new hypotheses or plans of action, and construct solutions to unfamiliar problems. Many Synthesis-level processes involve divergent thinking, thinking that can travel in many different directions, with no predetermined single correct answer. This is not to imply that there are no item guidelines, however, or that all student responses are acceptable. Indeed, the item should clearly and succinctly specify what is expected of the student.

The short-answer item is an excellent medium for sampling student creativity, a Synthesis-level component. You can use it to assess your students' skills at constructing original poetic compositions, as in this example:

Write a 5–7–5 haiku about spring.

Possible answer:

Spring comes once each year

Dressed in green and white and pink

To start life anew.

Synthesis-level in that it promotes creativity, this item has definite standards ("5–7–5 haiku about spring"). It is your responsibility to establish the point value of the item based on creativity, syllabication, originality, and so on. For instance, you could allow as many as four points for creativity, up to five points for the correct syllabication, and a maximum of three points for originality.

Evaluation Level: Students are required to make value judgments based on predetermined criteria or internal consistency. Remember that predetermined criteria are often personal, based on likes, dislikes, strengths, weaknesses, and so on and that there can be no predetermined correct answer. Rather, the correctness of an answer should be assessed according to the supporting rationale.

To assess your students' evaluations of literary personalities, short-answer items like the following are suitable.

Whom do you believe has the stronger will: Lady Macbeth or Scarlett O'Hara? List two (2) reasons to support your position.

Possible answer: I think Scarlett is, because

1. she remains strong, but Lady Macbeth becomes weaker as the play progresses.

2. Scarlett did long, hard, physical work, but Lady Macbeth probably would not have, even if it were necessary.

This is an Evaluation-level item because it necessitates value judgments, which you must score based on the rationale for the position rather than the position itself, even though the structure of the short-answer item precludes a detailed explanation. With respect to the sample response, the student's first reason is relatively strong; however, the second reason is based on conjecture. You could provide up to four points for each item, depending on evidence from the books and the strength of the student's logic.

ESSAY ITEMS, CONTENT AREAS, AND COGNITIVE DOMAIN LEVELS

A well-constructed essay item allows for an analytic examination of task-specific assignments, and it serves as a vehicle for the assessment of both creative and persuasive expression at the Analysis, Synthesis, and Evaluation levels. (To assess performance at the Knowledge, Comprehension, and Application levels, we recommend that you select from among the previously discussed test items.)

Mathematics

Analysis Level: Students are able to break a unified whole into its basic parts and understand the relationship among those parts, compare and contrast phenomena, understand metaphors and analogies, understand the relationship between cause and effect, and categorize phenomena.

To present your students with a problem necessitating a Venn diagram, which they would construct and analyze by explaining the inter-relationships among the subsets, you can use an essay item like the following:

> In a class of 360 students, 125 are enrolled in chemistry, 240 are enrolled in Spanish I, and 100 are taking both classes. How many students are taking either chemistry or Spanish I? (1) Construct a Venn diagram that shows the different enrollments, (2) determine how many students are taking either chemistry or Spanish I, and (3) *explain* (a) how you constructed the Venn diagram and (b) how you arrived at the number of students enrolled in either class. Make certain that you explain every step in each process and that you explain how the subsets are related.

The task-specific rubrics for this Analysis-level item should first address the construction of the Venn diagram, showing the three enrollments. The point value could range from 0 to 6. Next, the analytic rubrics should specify exactly how many students should be mentioned as taking either chemistry or Spanish I. The point value could possibly range from 0 to 6. Last, the rubrics should be structured to assess students' explanations of the Venn diagram construction and how they determined the number of students enrolled in the two classes. The point value could range from 0 to 6. Moreover, the rubrics should be structured to assess the presence of detail in the descriptions of each of the steps in the process. The points here could range from 0 to 6.

Synthesis Level: Students are able to assemble parts into a new whole, formulate new hypotheses or plans of action, and construct solutions to unfamiliar problems.

At the end of a statistics unit, you could determine your students' ability to create situations in which specific formulae would be appropriate by using an essay item, an excellent means for making such a determination. For instance,

> Within two paragraphs, create and explain an *original* problem in which the Chi-square statistical technique would be most appropriate for the problem's solution, and in your narrative, include two reasons why this technique would be most appropriate.

This Synthesis-level item requires students' individual creation of a hypothetical problem. In determining your rubric values, you could provide a minimum of three points for the originality and appropriateness of the problem, as many as three points for each of the supporting reasons, and as high as three points for organization and clarity.

Evaluation Level: Students should be able to make value judgments on the basis of predetermined criteria or internal consistency.

Proof of a mathematical statement can take several forms, and deciding which method of proof to employ can be a value judgment based on students' personally predetermined criteria. You can use essay items such as the following to assess your students' reasoning for selecting a particular method of proof.

Consider the following statement. "If $x > 2$, then x is not a rational number."

Within two to three paragraphs, explain whether you would use a direct or an indirect proof with this statement. In your explanation, include three reasons for your choice. You will be assessed on the logic, accuracy, and organization of each of your reasons and on the overall continuity and clarity of your essay.

Evaluation-level in that it involves a value judgment regarding two methods of proof, this item is clear and specific in its instructions. Such clarity and specificity are conducive to the construction of clear and precise task-specific rubrics. For example, you could decide to allow for as many as five points for each of the three reasons, depending on accuracy, clarity and organization; a maximum of seven points for overall organization; and a total of three points for grammar, spelling, and general usage.

Science

Analysis Level: Students are able to break a unified whole into its basic parts and understand the relationship among those parts, compare and contrast phenomena, understand metaphors and analogies, understand the relationship between cause and effect, and categorize phenomena.

The essay test is an excellent means of assessing students' ability to compare and contrast phenomena, which is an integral part of the Analysis component of classifying. Hence, you can use this instrument to gauge your students' ability to distinguish among rocks observed in the lab, for instance.

Within two paragraphs, compare and contrast an igneous and a metamorphic rock. In your narrative, include two similarities and two differences.

Analysis-level in that it involves comparing and contrasting, this item begins with a task-directed statement. The phrase "within two paragraphs" makes clear that this is an essay rather than a short-answer item, and the phrase "In your narrative" reinforces that this is to be an explanation rather than a listing. We suggest that your task-specific rubrics include a credit value that ranges from one to three points for each similarity and each difference, depending on the depth and breadth of the explanations.

Synthesis Level: Students are able to assemble parts into a new whole, formulate new hypotheses or plans of action, and construct solutions to unfamiliar problems.

You can use an essay item to assess students' ingenuity, for instance, in planning for the construction of practical devices with ordinary materials.

> Within two paragraphs, explain how you would use two single newspaper pages, one shoe box, four inches of duct tape, and one pair of scissors to construct an insulator for a soda can. You must use each of the items, and be sure that your explanation is clear and precise.

This Synthesis-level item calls for the students to exercise their creativity. Also, the specificity of this task-directed item allows for a clearly defined and effective analytic rubric. You could set a maximum of three points each for the use of the specified items, as many as five points for the functionality of the device, and up to three points for organization and clarity of the explanation.

Evaluation Level: Students should be able to make value judgments on the basis of predetermined criteria or internal consistency.

Environmental issues, often sources of controversy, can serve as the bases for value judgments. You can use essay items such as the one that follows as a means of assessing your students' ability to choose one particular side of an issue on the basis of factual logic.

> You have read several opposing articles concerning drilling for oil in Alaska. Within three paragraphs, explain whether you support the environmentalists' or the industrialists' point of view on this issue. In your narrative, include three points from your reading assignment that support your position. You will be assessed on the clarity, logic, and organization of your explanation.

With its call for a value judgment based on predetermined criteria, this item is clear in its requirements, and this clarity is conducive to the construction of precise analytic rubrics. For example, you could award as many as five points for each supporting reason, depending on clarity, detail, and reasonableness; a total of three points for clarity; as many as three points for logic; and a total of three points for organization.

Social Studies

Analysis Level: Students are able to break a unified whole into its basic parts and understand the relationship among those parts, compare and contrast phenomena, understand metaphors and analogies, understand the relationship between cause and effect, and categorize phenomena.

Objectively comparing and contrasting phenomena to understand similarities and differences between them is an Analysis-level task. You can use an essay item to determine the extent to which your students are able to discern that there are both commonalities and unique differences, for instance, between two great historical thinkers, as in this example.

> Within two to three pages, compare and contrast the ideas of John Adams and Alexander Hamilton. Within your analysis, include one similarity and one difference relating to each of the following: origins, purpose, and activities.

Analysis-level in that it involves comparing and contrasting two person's ideas, the item is direct and specific in what is expected of the students. Also, the phrases "Within two pages" and "Within your analysis" provide for an essay rather than a short-answer response. The clarity of the item lends itself to task-specific rubrics. For example, you could assign a maximum of three and a minimum of one point for each similarity and difference relating to origins, purposes, and activities.

Synthesis Level: Students are able to assemble parts into a new whole, formulate new hypotheses or plans of action, and construct solutions to unfamiliar problems.

Labor–management disagreements are virtually continual, and their resolutions usually involve compromise. You could use an essay item effectively to assess your students' creative skills in drafting a labor–management agreement such as the following.

> Assume that as a member of an arbitrating team, you must decide on a health care plan for employees whose health benefits have always been paid for by a company that is now operating in the red and now demands that employees assume full financial responsibility for their health care insurance. However, the employees demand that the company continue to pay all of their health insurance costs.

> Within two pages, draft a three-year proposal that both sides can tolerate. Include in your proposal (1) one compromise and (2) two contingencies with (a) one supporting reason for the compromise and (b) one supporting reason for each of the two contingencies.

This task-directed item calls for a high level of creativity from the students. It is also conducive to an individually tailored rubric. For instance, you could establish a maximum of five points for the compromise and as many as three points for the rationale supporting it, a total of four points for each contingency, and up to three points for the supporting reason for each.

Evaluation Level: Students should be able to make value judgments on the basis of predetermined criteria or internal consistency.

More often than not, appropriations within the federal budget are sources of value conflicts. You can use an essay item to assess your students' skills in making value judgments, for instance, about federal monetary appropriations, as in the next example.

> In comparison to the federal monies that are being appropriated for the military, do you think more money should be spent on education? In two to three paragraphs, explain whether you agree or disagree and include three factual reasons to support your position. You will be assessed on the logic and organization of each of your three reasons; the overall clarity of your essay; and grammar, spelling, and general mechanics.

This Evaluation-level item, requiring a value judgment, cautions against an emotional choice with its instruction to "include three factual reasons." Also, in addition to defining exactly what is expected of the students, the specificity of the item is conducive to the easy construction of analytic rubrics. For example, you could assign a maximum of six points, depending on accuracy and detail, for each of the three reasons; seven points for overall organization, clarity, and continuity; and five points for grammar, spelling, capitalization, and other mechanical usages.

English–Language Arts

Analysis Level: Students are able to break a unified whole into its basic parts and understand the relationship among those parts, compare and contrast phenomena, understand metaphors and analogies, understand the relationship between cause and effect, and categorize phenomena.

The process of understanding literary symbolism is an analytic endeavor. You can use essay items to assess your students' ability to uncover symbolic meaning from their assigned readings, as in the following example.

Within two paragraphs, explain what the albatross in the *Rime of the Ancient Mariner* symbolizes. In your explanation, include three examples from the story that substantiate your position.

In this Analysis-level item, students must first determine the phenomenon that the albatross symbolizes. Then they must provide three textual examples to support their deduction. With respect to scoring the item, your task-specific rubric could contain up to five points for the phenomenon symbolized by the albatross; from zero to four points could be earned for each of the three supporting examples, depending on accuracy and detail; and one to three points could be assigned for organization.

Synthesis Level: Students are able to assemble parts into a new whole, formulate new hypotheses or plans of action, and construct solutions to unfamiliar problems.

Creative writing is an important aspect of students' literary development, and you can use essay items to assess your students' literary creativity. Also, specifications within an essay item can provide rather than restrict opportunities for creativity, as in the following example:

Within two pages, write a short story that contains two main characters, as many supplementary characters as you wish, one action event, and a surprise ending. You will be assessed on originality, organization, the specified components, grammar, mechanics, and to some extent, spelling.

This Synthesis-level item provides for a breadth of creativity while simultaneously providing for the construction of analytic rubrics. For example, you could assign a maximum of five points for the student's portrayal of each of the main characters, up to five points for the total treatment of the supplementary personalities, as many as four points for the action event, four total points for the ending, up to four points for originality, a maximum of three points for grammar, three for mechanics, and two for spelling.

Evaluation Level: Students should be able to make value judgments on the basis of predetermined criteria or internal consistency.

All literary critics, both professional and amateur, have their preferences for authors' treatments of various issues. You can use essay items to assess your students' ability to make value judgments pertaining to different authors' approaches, for instance, to given social phenomena, as in this example:

> Explain in two or three paragraphs whether you prefer Faulkner's or Caldwell's treatment of the rural poor. In your narrative, include three examples from the text to support your position. You will be assessed on the organization, accuracy, and clarity of each of your three supporting reasons; the overall continuity and clarity of your paper; and the grammar, spelling, and general mechanics in your essay.

Evaluation-level with its requirement for a value judgment regarding two authors' treatments of a mutual subject, the item specifically states what is expected of the student, which makes for clearly defined analytical rubrics. For instance, you could allow a maximum of six points for each of the three supporting reasons, with respect to organization, accuracy, and clarity; seven points for the essay's general clarity and continuity; and five points for grammar, spelling, and general mechanics.

SUMMARY

Short-Answer Item

Some measurement specialists equate the short-answer with the completion item, perceiving each as confined to the Knowledge level, and some make no distinction between the structures of the two items. As we have demonstrated, however, the short-answer item can be an effective vehicle for measurement in each of the cognitive levels within the major content areas. As either a question or a command, this item is a useful device for measuring both convergent and divergent thinking. The items must indicate exactly what is expected of the students, however, so that you are confident that the students' responses are true indicators of what they actually know. Nevertheless, as always, the items should contain no hints or clues to the correct answers.

Essay Item

The essay item has definite strengths as well as pronounced limitations. A primary strength is its allowance for a detailed, in-depth analysis of a small area of focus. Moreover, it permits the assessment of the students' analytical, organizational, and creative skills. Hence, the item should be employed at the Analysis, Synthesis, and Evaluation levels, leaving assessment at the first three levels to some of the other types of test items. If you wish to cover broad areas of material, forgo the essay item in favor of one of the other types, especially the multiple-choice item, if it is your intent to test students at the Knowledge, Comprehension, Application, or Analysis levels.

As always, the item should specify precisely what is expected of the students to ensure that they understand what is expected of them; it also makes for an easily constructed and task-specific rubric. Even with clearly defined rubrics, it is important that you grade essays item by item as opposed to paper by paper. With this procedure, you are grading the papers more anonymously—grading papers rather than people.

PROFESSIONAL DEVELOPMENT ACTIVITIES

1. Divide into groups according to content areas. After reviewing the guidelines for constructing the short-answer item, review the definitions of the cognitive levels. Now collectively construct a short-answer item in your content area for each of the following levels:

   a. Knowledge

   b. Comprehension

   c. Application

   d. Analysis

   e. Synthesis

   f. Evaluation

Compare your items with those in the chapter. Then have members from all the groups put their Knowledge-level items on the board for discussion. When you have completed the discussion, follow the same procedure for the remaining five levels.

2. In content-area groups, review the guidelines for constructing the essay item and review the definitions of the cognitive levels. Now collectively construct an essay item in your content area for each of the following levels:

   a. Analysis

   b. Synthesis

   c. Evaluation

Be sure to construct task-specific rubrics for each item. Compare your items with those in the chapter. Have members from each group put their Analysis-level items on the board for discussion. When you have completed the discussion, follow the same procedure for the Synthesis and Evaluation levels.

WWW RESOURCES

http://www.wmich.edu/grad/gatraining/TAgetting1.htm
This Western Michigan University Web site offers instruction on the strengths, weaknesses, construction, preparation, and scoring of essay items.

http://www.pitt.edu/~ciddeweb/faculty-development/fds/testing2.html
This University of Pittsburgh Web site gives information regarding the strengths, weaknesses, uses, construction, and scoring of essay items.

6 Performance-Based Assessment

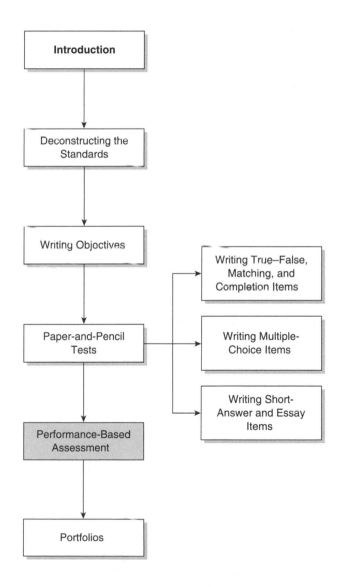

Introduction

Deconstructing the Standards

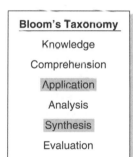

Bloom's Taxonomy
Knowledge
Comprehension
Application
Analysis
Synthesis
Evaluation

Writing Objectives

Paper-and-Pencil Tests

Writing True–False, Matching, and Completion Items

Writing Multiple-Choice Items

Writing Short-Answer and Essay Items

Performance-Based Assessment

Portfolios

Despite the power and versatility of paper-and-pencil tests, they cannot assess certain areas of pupil performance. For example, a student can write a description of a lab demonstration, list the steps for setting up a VCR for use, and explain the Heimlich maneuver, but the actual execution of these tasks can be appraised only through performance-based assessment, and such assessment can be applied to both processes and products of performance: *processes* are ongoing procedures leading to a final result, such as collecting sources and writing rough drafts enroute to a finished paper, whereas *products* are the culminating results accomplished through a series or sequence of procedures. For example, after deciding on a topic, your student will probably construct an outline describing the contents of a proposed paper. After you have returned the outline, the student would most likely write more than one draft before completing the paper. The outline and drafts are process procedures, and the final paper is the product.

Some student performances are restricted to one day, while others are extended over a span of time. A restricted performance is specifically defined and can be accomplished and observed during a single session, such as taking a wire, a light bulb, and a battery and then connecting them so that the bulb lights. An extended performance may take several days, or even longer, such as collecting and assembling plant parts for a classification display.

Many performance activities provide for the assessment of behavior that cannot be evaluated by paper-and-pencil tests, but the reliability (consistency of performance) and validity (actually measuring what you want them to measure) of these performances are sometimes difficult to determine. Hence, it is imperative that the purpose of the performance be established beforehand, along with whether it is to be restricted or extended and whether the emphasis is centered on process or product. Furthermore, you should specify exactly which materials, resources, and equipment are to be used. Most important are clearly defined expectations of your students' performances (see Chapter 2), because a high level of clarity is conducive to your students' understanding of what is expected of them, and it also makes for the easy construction of effective rubrics: The more clearly defined and focused the description and directions, the more effective the rubric as an assessment device. As mentioned in Chapter 5, generic rubrics serve a number of purposes. Yet since the performances in this chapter are in compliance with daily instructional objectives, they require analytical or task-specific rubrics.

CHECKLISTS AND RATING SCALES

Checklists and rating scales can assess your students' performances. A **checklist** usually provides for yes–no classifications:

Satisfactory = 1; Unsatisfactory = 0.

Yes = 1; No = 0.

A **rating scale** is a kind of continuum, usually ranging from zero to three, four, five, six, or seven:

3 = Always or very frequently

2 = Most of the time

1 = Sometimes

0 = Never

Regardless of whether you elect to use a checklist or a rating scale, the points that you award should be based on (1) performance objectives and (2) observable indicators.

Poor Checklist Objective: Students will know about the uniqueness of fingerprints. Yes = 1; No = 0

Since this objective does not provide for the observation of student behavior, you would probably have difficulty in accurately assessing your pupils' knowledge.

Good Checklist Objective: Presented with a blotter containing the index fingerprints of two classmates, students will list two differences between the two. Satisfactory = 1; Unsatisfactory = 0

Since this objective clearly specifies the desired performance, you are easily able to make an accurate assessment of your students' performance.

Poor Rating Scale Objective: Students will know the exports of given South American countries.

Very Well = 5 points

Well = 4 points

Fairly Well = 3 points

Not Very Well = 2 points

Poorly = 1 point

Very Poorly = 0 points

This objective does not specify how you are to determine the extent to which your students "know" (a very nebulous term) the exports of South American countries. Moreover, the entire rating scale is open to a multiplicity of interpretations.

Good Rating Scale Objective: As an Internet assignment, students will each research a South American country and list at least seven of that country's imports, with a Web site source.

7 = 5 points

6 = 4 points

5 = 3 points

3–4 = 2 points

1–2 = 1 point

0 = 0 points

Since this objective specifies the exact number of points to be awarded for correct list items, you will have no difficulty in accurately assessing your students' performances.

Holistic Scoring

There are instances when you may wish to implement holistic scoring, a procedure in which an overall score is assigned to the total performance, whether it is a project, a presentation, a paper, or whatever. Borich and Tombari (2004) use the following model as an example of a holistic rubric (see Table 6.1). A gymnastics judge may assign a score of 1–10 for a gymnastics performance. This type of assessment is known as *subjective scoring* because the single, awarded score represents multiple movements performed by the gymnast. Similarly, a teacher may assign a rubric score of 6 to a student's original poem, even though the poem is the product of a number of separate efforts. As Arter and McTighe (2001) mention, holistic scoring provides a "quick snapshot of overall status or achievement" (p. 25). However, they continue by acknowledging that analytical scoring is more detailed and specific.

Analytic Scoring

Analytic scoring is much more detailed than holistic scoring, lessening the opportunities for scoring biases. Remember, clearly defined performance

Table 6.1   Sample Grades and Categories for a Holistic Rubric

Rubric Score	Grade	Category
7	A+	Excellent
6	A	Excellent
5	B+	Good
4	B	Good
3	C+	Fair
2	C	Fair
1	D	Needs Improvement

Source: Borich and Tombari (2004, p. 217)

expectations (objectives) are conducive to detailed and clearly defined rubrics. As the examples in this chapter demonstrate, analytic scoring is better suited to more precise assessment of student performances in the classroom. The following noneducational example parallels the type of rubric that you could use for a classroom performance.

> Ms. Garcia and her son, Hector, agreed that Hector should assume responsibility for the family's dog. Ms. Garcia constructed the following weekly chart that includes wages that she chose arbitrarily, as if Hector were being paid. The two thought that Hector could use a couple of the scored weekly charts as references for future pet care jobs.

Table 6.2 represents the total amount Hector could potentially earn in a week. Table 6.3 shows the total amount Hector earned for the week of February 8–14, 2009.

> Although Hector's first week's performance was satisfactory, he and his mother feel that he can do better. He may later use his scored assessment, along with an improved future performance, as a process-oriented reference.

Performance-based assessments certainly have drawbacks and limitations: They often lack the reliability and validity found in paper-and pencil tests, they are time consuming, they often involve groups as opposed to individuals, and they lack the generalizability of traditional tests. Still,

Table 6.2 The Total Amount Hector Could Earn in a Week

	Monday		Tuesday		Wednesday		Thursday		Friday		Saturday		Sunday	
	AM	PM	AM	PM	AM	PM	AM	PM	AM	PM	AM	PM	AM	PM
Feed	$0.30	$0.30	$0.30	$0.30	$0.30	$0.30	$0.30	$0.30	$0.30	$0.30	$0.30	$0.30	$0.30	$0.30
Water	$0.30	$0.30	$0.30	$0.30	$0.30	$0.30	$0.30	$0.30	$0.30	$0.30	$0.30	$0.30	$0.30	$0.30
15–20 min. walk	$0.50	$0.50	$0.50	$0.50	$0.50	$0.50	$0.50	$0.50	$0.50	$0.50	$0.50	$0.50	$0.50	$0.50
10–14 min. walk	$0.30	$0.30	$0.30	$0.30	$0.30	$0.30	$0.30	$0.30	$0.30	$0.30	$0.30	$0.30	$0.30	$0.30
5–9 min. walk	$0.10	$0.10	$0.10	$0.10	$0.10	$0.10	$0.10	$0.10	$0.10	$0.10	$0.10	$0.10	$0.10	$0.10
Groom	$0.15	$0.15	$0.15	$0.15	$0.15	$0.15	$0.15	$0.15	$0.15	$0.15	$0.15	$0.15	$0.15	$0.15
Total possible per day		$3.30		$3.30		$3.30		$3.30		$3.30		$3.30		$3.30
Total possible per week		$23.10												

Table 6.3   The Amount Hector Actually Earned in One Week

February 8–14, 2009

	Monday		Tuesday		Wednesday		Thursday		Friday		Saturday		Sunday	
	AM	PM	AM	PM	AM	PM	AM	PM	AM	PM	AM	PM	AM	PM
Feed	$0.30	$0.30	$0.30	$0.30	$0.30	$0.30	$0.30	$0.30	$0.30	$0.30	$0.30	$0.30	$0.30	$0.30
Water	$0.30	$0.30	$0.30	$0.30	$0.30	$0.30	$0.30	$0.30	$0.30	$0.30	$0.30	$0.30	$0.30	$0.30
15–20 min. walk	$0.50				$0.50	$0.50		$0.50				$0.50		$0.50
10–14 min. walk		$0.30	$0.30						$0.30	$0.30		$0.30		
5–9 min. walk		$0.10		$0.10			$0.10				$0.10		$0.10	
Groom	$0.15	$0.15	$0.15	$0.15	$0.15	$0.15	$0.15	$0.15	$0.15	$0.15	$0.15	$0.15	$0.15	$0.15
Total possible per day		$3.30		$3.30		$3.30		$3.30		$3.30		$3.30		$3.30
Total earned per day		$2.30		$1.90		$2.50		$2.10		$2.10		$2.40		$2.10
Total possible per week	$23.10													
Total earned for week of February 8–14, 2009	$15.40													

performance-based assessment is a necessary component of any assessment program because it is the only method of discerning hands-on abilities.

There is a direct relationship between the importance that you place on a performance and the complexity of your students' performances: the more important the performance, the greater the number of its components. Hence, the importance of the performance determines the point value of the rubric. For example, major performances, such as the English–language arts example and the social studies example in the upcoming pages, require multiple-component rubrics, whereas less complex performances, such as the mathematics example on page 107, require fewer dimensions. The following examples demonstrate how to implement performance-based assessment within the major content areas.

EXAMPLES BY CONTENT AREA

Mathematics

Let's say you want your students to apply (Application) some of their geometrical formulae in authentic situations creatively (Synthesis). In your objective, you should define exactly what you expect of your students and then design analytical rubrics that can assess their performance. This is a *divergent* task, which involves thinking that can go in multiple directions.

Objective

In groups of two or three, students will use four geometric formulae in their plans for the construction of the shell of a 20' × 40' building, which will also include a roof of their choice, a gutter on each side, and two rain spouts.

Although this objective calls for the application of geometric formulae, it provides for a creative application, with performance at the Synthesis level being dependent on mastery of the Application level. Table 6.4 is a sample rubric that could apply to this task.

These task-specific rubrics, directed toward the assessment of an extended group performance, provide maximum points for each component. The rubrics provide certain leeway for your professional judgment, which you should exercise with caution and objectivity, especially since this is a group project, which is a further threat to objective assessment. Even though the group members most likely did not contribute equally to the project, you would probably assign the same grade to each of the members rather than risk penalizing someone unjustly.

Table 6.4

Criteria	Maximum Points	Points Earned
Exact dimension of the shell	4	
Inclusion of all four geometrical formulae (2 points for each inclusion)	8	
Suitability of fit among the four formulae (judgment decision)	5	
Functional and aesthetic qualities of the roof (attractiveness and function)	5	
Inclusion of each gutter (1 point per gutter)	2	
Inclusion of each rainspout (1 point per rain spout)	2	
Functional placement of each rainspout (function)	2	
Overall appearance of the shell (judgment)	5	
Overall function of the shell (workability)	5	
Possible Points	38	

Science

During a unit on acids and bases, you could engage your students in an actual, real-life experience of determining the acid composition of an unknown liquid, as described in the example that follows. This kind of activity involves *convergent thinking,* which leads to conventionally accepted best answers or predetermined right answers (e.g., the actual acid composition).

Objective

Presented with a beaker containing an unknown liquid, a pH meter, and a paper towel, students will sequentially demonstrate the three previously presented safety rules while measuring and then recording the acid content of the liquid within one 100th of a milliliter.

This is an Application-level objective in that students must actually demonstrate (apply) something that was previously presented to them. Also, it specifies an exact degree of accuracy ("within one 100th of a milliliter").

The point value of any analytical rubric is left to your professional discretion, depending on the emphasis you give to each aspect of the performance. The following is a suggestion.

Table 6.5

Criteria	Maximum Points	Points Earned
Following the three safety rules in sequence	6	
Including each safety rule but not in sequence	3	
Recording exact measurement	10	
Recording within .01 of the exact measurement	9	
Recording within .02 of the exact measurement	8	
Recording within .03 of the exact measurement	7	
Recording within .04 of the exact measurement	6	
Recording within .05 of the exact measurement	5	
Recording within .06 of the exact measurement	4	
Recording within .07 of the exact measurement	3	
Recording within .08 of the exact measurement	2	
Recording within .09 of the exact measurement	1	
Maximum points possible	16	

Social Studies

Let's say you assemble your students into small cooperative groups for the purpose of designing hypothetical peace plans for an actual international conflict. The following objective would be pertinent and involves *divergent thinking* (traveling in many different directions).

Objective

In groups of two or three, students will research and then design a peace proposal between two countries in conflict currently in the news, which will include three compromises from each group, presented in a three- to four-page type-written report.

This is a Synthesis-level objective, requiring students to undertake research to serve as the basis for their cooperative creation of a peace plan that will necessitate compromises from both parties.

With such an extended and group-oriented project, the emphasis of the assessment should be on product rather than process. Table 6.6 is a set of suggested rubrics.

The specificity of the objective lends itself to these analytical rubrics, which provides for assessment of each of the suggested compromises,

Table 6.6

Criteria		Points		Points		Points		Points
Compromise 1: Pertinence	Critically important to both sides	5	Mildly important to both sides	3–4	Not very important; easily resolved	1–2	Unimportant issue	0
Compromise 1: Balance between relinquishing and receiving	Delicately balanced; neither side relinquishes more than it receives	5	Slightly tilted toward one side, which receives slightly more than it relinquishes	3–4	Heavily tilted toward one side, which receives much more than it relinquishes	1–2	Almost totally favoring one side	0
Compromise 2: Pertinence	Critically important to both sides	5	Mildly important to both sides	3–4	Not very important; easily resolved	1–2	Unimportant issue	0
Compromise 2: Balance between relinquishing and receiving	Delicately balanced; neither side relinquishes more than it receives	5	Slightly tilted toward one side, which receives slightly more than it relinquishes	3–4	Heavily tilted toward one side, which receives much more than it relinquishes	1–2	Almost totally favoring one side	0
Compromise 3: Pertinence	Virtually important to both sides	5	Mildly important to both sides	3–4	Not very important; easily resolved	1–2	Unimportant issue	0

(Continued)

Table 6.6 (Continued)

Criteria		Points		Points		Points		Points
Compromise 3: Balance between relinquishing and receiving	Delicately balanced; neither side relinquishes more than it receives	5	Slightly tilted toward one side, which receives slightly more than it relinquishes	3–4	Heavily tilted toward one side, which receives much more than it relinquishes	1–2	Almost totally favoring one side, which receives more than it relinquishes	0
Organization	Logically organized in a step-by-step sequence, with each step building on the previous step	5	Somewhat organized, but not necessary sequentially	3–4	Noticeably unorganized; patterns are difficult to discern	1–2	Very disorganized; no continuity	0
Grammar, Punctuation, Capitalization, Spelling	No more than three errors	5	Four to five errors	3–4	Six to seven errors	1–2	More than eight errors	0
	Maximum Possible Points	40	Points earned					

along with the page limitations, organization and clarity, and the general mechanics of the proposal. Since it is a group performance, however, there is no assurance that the across-the-group score will reflect equal contributions by each of the group members.

English–Language Arts

Creative writing assignments with mandatory guidelines can enhance rather than stifle creativity in that they encourage the students to be creative in ways that they may have overlooked otherwise. With this in mind, you may have your students write a short story that includes elements of prescribed creativity.

Objective

As a class assignment, students will each write a short story, within two to three pages, that contains two credible main characters, one credible supporting character, an action event, and a surprise ending.

This is a Synthesis-level objective, motivating the students to exercise and expand their creative skills. Since this assignment is designed to be completed within a single class period, it is an individual and restricted performance, whose product rather than process is the focus of assessment. However, you may want to collect your students' rough drafts to determine how they arrived at their completed products. In any event, the analytical rubric on page 112 is one suggestion.

Remember that since this is an in-class assignment, students are subject to pressures of time; hence, you should not score the papers as critically as you would if they were out-of-class assignments.

SUMMARY

Performance-based assessment is applied to skills and abilities that cannot be evaluated by traditional paper-and-pencil tests. This method of assessment can target process or product and time-restricted or time-extended activities. Like other forms of assessment, this one has definite strengths as well as pronounced weaknesses.

For scoring, although generic rubric models are valuable, tailoring your rubrics to individual performances, as detailed in your daily instructional objectives, allows for more precise evaluation. In this type of assessment, as in others, clearly defined objectives make for easy construction of objective and detailed rubrics that minimize scoring subjectivity.

Table 6.7

Criteria		Points		Points		Points		Points
Main Character A: Description and involvement	Believable, detailed characteristics; very important role involvement	5	Somewhat believable; relatively important role involvement	3–4	Not very believable; little mention of characteristics; not very important role involvement	1–2	Unrealistic; no mention of personal characteristics; unimportant role involvement	0
Main Character B: Description and involvement	Believable, detailed characteristics; very important role involvement	5	Somewhat believable; relatively important role involvement	3–4	Not very believable; little mention of characteristics; not very important role involvement	1–2	Unrealistic; no mention of personal characteristics; unimportant role involvement	0
Supporting Character	Believable, detailed characteristics; very important supporting involvement	5	Somewhat believable; mention of characteristics; relatively important and supporting involvement	3–4	Not very believable; little mention of characteristics; not very important supporting role involvement	1–2	Unrealistic; little mention of personal characteristics; unimportant supporting role involvement	0

Criteria	Points		Points		Points		Points		Points
Action Event	5	Very descriptive and exciting	3–4	Somewhat descriptive; somewhat exciting	1–2	Little description; hardly exciting	0	No description; boring; anticipated	
Surprise Ending	5	Very surprising; unexpected; detailed description	3–4	Relatively surprising, but somewhat expected; some detail in description	1–2	Not very surprising; hardly unexpected; little detail in description	0	Not surprising; expected; no detail in description	
Organization, Continuity, Flow	5	Flows in logical, step-by-step sequence	3–4	Some continuity and flow; relatively logical, with partially sequential events	1–2	Little continuity or flow; somewhat logical; little planned direction; difficult to follow	0	No continuity or flow; illogical; no perceivable pattern of events	
Grammar, Punctuation, Capitalization, Spelling	5	No more than three errors	3–4	4–5 errors	1–2	6–7 errors	0	More than eight grammatical errors	
	35	Maximum Points		Points Earned					

PROFESSIONAL DEVELOPMENT ACTIVITIES

In groups of three or four according to content areas, construct performance-based activities either for individuals or for groups. Once you have determined these activities, begin constructing the rubric. If you have questions, refer to the chapter examples. Make sure you know the cognitive level of your activities. After completion, put every group's items on the board for discussion.

WWW RESOURCES

http://www.aurbach.com/alt_assess.html
This Web site defines various types of performance-based assessment, along with their respective components.

http://www.miamisci.org/ph/lpdefine.html
The University of Miami Web site offers real-world challenges for cooperative or individual completion of authentic project and tasks, along with suggestions for assessing student performances.

Many generic rubrics are available on the Web, as are sources of technology assessment, some of which are listed in Table 6.8.

Table 6.8 Web Sites That Contain Examples of Generic Rubrics

Assess and Report Progress	http://www.metiri.com/8steps/STEPeightRubrics.htm
Discovery Channel School	http://school.discovery.com/schrockguide/assess.html
teAchnology	http://www/teach-nology.com/web_tools/rubrics/rubrics.htm
Education Service Center Region 20	http://www.esc20.k12.tx.us/etprojects/rubrics/Default.htm
MyTeacherTools.com	http://www.rubrics4teachers.com/>
Secondary School Educators	http://712educators.about.com/cs/rubrics/a/rubrics.htm
University of Wisconsin-Stout	http://www.uwstout.edu/soe/profdev/rubrics.shtml
The WebQuest Page	http://webquest.sdsu.edu/
PALS: Tasks	http://pals.sri.com/tasks/

7

Portfolios

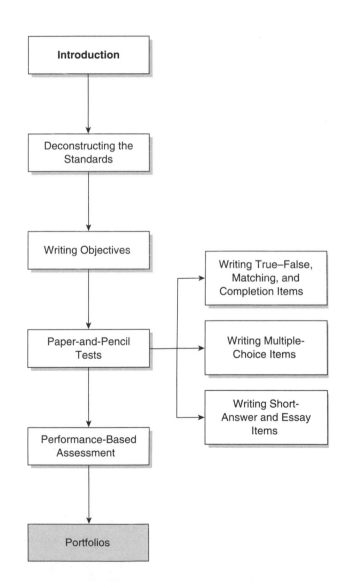

Introduction

Deconstructing the Standards

Bloom's Taxonomy
- Knowledge
- Comprehension
- Application
- Analysis
- Synthesis
- Evaluation

Writing Objectives

Writing True–False, Matching, and Completion Items

Paper-and-Pencil Tests

Writing Multiple-Choice Items

Writing Short-Answer and Essay Items

Performance-Based Assessment

Portfolios

The portfolio can be a highly effective device for exhibiting both the processes and the products of student efforts. Nevertheless, many educators insist that there are two distinct types of portfolios: those that evidence pupil progress (growth) and those that show the students' best efforts (showcase). In this chapter, we demonstrate that a single portfolio can serve as both a growth chart and a showcase, without requiring a warehouse for its storage.

The contents of a portfolio should include representative samples of a student's performance within each of the levels of the cognitive hierarchy within a particular content area. It should display selected representative examples of pupil processes that led to demonstrated accomplishments within each of the levels of a cognitive hierarchy. To ensure that the display reflects curricular content as well as performances within each of the cognitive levels, you could also include unit and daily instructional objectives and test and performance-based assessment results.

Encourage your students to participate in the selection of their portfolio entries and stress the importance of representing their growth. Hence, the portfolio should show not only finished products but also the sequential steps leading to them. Note that presenting only a student's best or worst work provides a misrepresentation, which can be prevented through teacher guidance.

Once portfolios have been assembled, set aside time for your students to review them and then write and enter their reflections for later review. Although these reflections can be time consuming, they can provide valuable insight into your students' reactions to their academic involvements. Also, regularly set aside time for teacher–student conferences to discuss the progress that your students have achieved to date. Such pupil involvement is designed to allow the students to assess their own learning and enable them to assume ownership of their learning as well. Moreover, whether the portfolios are housed in folders or electronically, the students should work with you in dating and categorizing the material according to topic, cognitive level, and process-to-product sequence, in compliance with national or state standards (Chapter 1). Furthermore, the students should construct tables of contents both for their own use and for teacher–student and parent–teacher conferences. Box 7.1 contains a vignette regarding a portfolio's development.

Box 7.1

In conference with Miranda, Mr. Zatopec has suggested including a corrected rough draft of her term paper in her portfolio. Miranda asserts that this version does not represent her best work. Agreeing, her teacher reminds her that a portfolio should reflect process and growth. He explains that this rough draft will become more meaningful when compared with the final version, which could be included later. Miranda agrees.

When portfolios contain an overabundance of your students' work, they become less meaningful. By inserting carefully selected representative samples of the students' performances according to the cognitive hierarchy, you, your students, and their parents can better understand the students' areas of cognitive strengths and weaknesses. Box 7.2 contains a vignette showing the use of a portfolio in a parent conference.

Box 7.2

In a meeting with Ms. Fong, Jamal Washington's father says that he is puzzled because his son did not have an A on his interim report, especially after receiving near-perfect scores on all of his spelling, labeling, and definition exercises, as well as a high score on an in-class opinion paper. After the two of them review Jamal's portfolio, which is arranged by date and cognitive level, Mr. Washington understands that although Jamal is making progress, he still needs to work on his Comprehension-, Application-, and Synthesis-level skills.

Rather than using traditional portfolio containers, you may wish to enter your students' work samples electronically. (The WWW Resources section at the end of the chapter provides Web resources for electronic portfolios.) Electronic portfolios can include graphics as well as video and sound, and they are easily accessible. Moreover, meaningful connections among different subject matter areas can be made.

CONTENT AREAS, COGNITIVE LEVELS, AND PORTFOLIO ENTRIES

The following examples demonstrate how your unit and daily instructional objectives can serve as guidelines for the selection of appropriate and representative portfolio artifacts. We use a number of examples that were employed in Chapter 2. For performance-based activities, you and your students can choose from among the scored rubrics of completed tasks (see Chapter 6). A sample objective is cited at each cognitive level with a corresponding artifact suggested for the portfolios.

Mathematics

Knowledge Level: Students can recognize and recall previously learned information; no comprehension or understanding of the information is implied.

You and your students will want to select from among activities within this level as a starting point for displaying their progression through the cognitive hierarchy of the curriculum. For instance, in accordance with your unit and daily instructional objectives, you and your student could select a portfolio entry from among tasks that involved Knowledge-level performance that demonstrates your student's knowledge of geometrical formulae.

Sample Daily Instructional Objective: On a worksheet containing the names of five geometrical figures, students will write the formula for computing the area of each.

If selected as a representative Knowledge-level artifact, you and your student could enter an example that did not meet the objective's standards, as an example of process. An example that met the standards could be entered as a completed product.

Comprehension Level: Students are able to understand or summarize information, translate information from one form or level to another, and comprehend data trends.

At the Comprehension level, the student is to demonstrate understanding of phenomena, which goes beyond simple memorization but stops short of actual application. Such performances could be a consideration for portfolio work samples.

Sample Daily Instructional Objective: In the provided spaces on a worksheet containing five descriptive statistics problems, students will write the formula for computing each.

Depending on the level of performance on this daily instructional objective, you and your student may decide to use the scored worksheet as either a process-oriented or a product-oriented work sample.

Application Level: Students have the ability to take information that has previously been acquired and comprehended and use it in concrete situations.

As a part of a unit on central tendency, you can determine how well your students apply various formulae to actual statistics problems. Then, you and your student may consider the scored results of the efforts as a possible Application-level artifact in the student's portfolio.

Sample Daily Instructional Objective: Presented with fifty random numbers, the students will compute their mean and median to two decimal places.

An Application-level assignment in that it requires applying previously acquired formulae, you and your student may wish to consider the scored results as either a process or product portfolio artifact.

Analysis Level: Students are able to break down a unified whole into its basic parts and understand the relationship among these parts, determine cause–effect relationships, understand analogies and metaphors, and categorize phenomena.

You and your student can consider the scored results of a daily classroom exercise as a representative sample of daily performance on Analysis-level assignments.

Sample Daily Instructional Objective: As a classroom exercise, students will construct a Venn diagram to solve the following problem: In a class of 320 students, if 85 students are taking chemistry, 200 are taking English, and 60 are taking both classes, how many students are taking either chemistry or English?

Analysis-level in that the student must determine relationships, the scored drawing can be considered by the two of you as a growth-related sample.

Synthesis Level: Students are able to assemble parts into a whole, formulate new hypotheses or plans of action, and construct solutions to unfamiliar problems.

When your students are able to apply the formulae and theorems that they have recently studied, you can give them the opportunity to be creative with the formulae and theorems. Then you and your student may want to examine these creative efforts for consideration as possible process or product portfolio work samples.

Sample Daily Instructional Objective: As a classroom assignment, students will construct and solve a word problem that necessitates an application of the Pythagorean theorem for its solution.

Since the standards of this objective involve both Synthesis- and Application-level performances, the rubrics should provide for the assessment of both levels. Then you and your student may want to consider the scored rubric as either a process or product portfolio artifact.

Evaluation Level: Students are able to make value judgments on the basis of predetermined criteria or internal consistency. Since value judgments often involve personal choices, you should assess the students' rationale for their decisions as opposed to their decisions per se.

Theorems lend themselves to various methods of proof, and why students select one method as opposed to others is a value judgment that is often based on personal preference, which may reflect a comfort level with a particular method, as in the example to follow. Knowing this may help you enhance your students' mathematics performance. Then you and your student can decide whether to include a scored assessment as a portfolio work sample.

Sample Daily Instructional Objective: Presented with two theorems, students will select a method of proof (direct, contrapositive, or contradictory) to apply to each, and then write two reasons for each of their choices.

Both you and your student should examine the scored paper for possible entry into the portfolio, probably as a process-level inclusion, keeping in mind that the paper could be an excellent reference for both parent and student conferences.

Science

Knowledge Level: Students are expected to recognize and recall previously learned information; no comprehension or understanding of the information is implied.

You and your students will want to select from among activities within this level to establish a starting point for their progression through the cognitive hierarchy of this curriculum. Sometimes you and your student may agree on a daily quiz as a representative sample for portfolio entry.

Sample Daily Instructional Objective: On a ten-item quiz of the chemical elements, students will write the corresponding symbol beside at least eight.

If this paper-and-pencil performance is mutually agreed on, you and your student may opt to include the corrected quiz—as a process artifact if the standards were not met and as a product if they were.

Comprehension Level: Students are able to understand or summarize information, translate information from one form or level to another, and comprehend data trends.

An understanding of observed lab demonstrations is fundamental to the actual conducting of supervised demonstrations or experiments, and you can have your students observe and record their observations of teacher-conducted lab demonstrations.

Sample Daily Instructional Objective: Following an observed laboratory demonstration, students will summarize the demonstration by listing (a) each of the three pieces of equipment used and (b) the three-step process of the demonstration, in sequence.

You and your student may decide to include a graded summary of observations as a portfolio work sample or possibly as a source of comparison for future experiments conducted by the student.

Application Level: Students are able to take information that has previously been acquired and comprehended and use it in concrete situations.

The ability to use scientific instruments to solve problems is essential to many laboratory performances. A student's recorded assessment of performance could be considered by the two of you as a possible Application-level entry for the portfolio.

Sample Daily Instructional Objective: As a lab exercise, students will use colorimeters to determine the specific gravity of an unknown sample, within 0.2 units.

Depending on the student's level of performance, the two of you could consider the recorded assessment as either a representative growth- or product-oriented Application-level work sample for the portfolio.

Analysis Level: Students are able to break down a unified whole into its basic parts and understand the relationship among these parts, determine cause–effect relationships, understand analogies and metaphors, and categorize phenomena.

The ability to compare and contrast phenomena is an Analysis-level activity. The following example would apply to determine your students' abilities to distinguish among different rock types.

Sample Daily Instructional Objective: Given the terms *Triassic and Permian* geologic time periods, students will correctly list two similarities and two differences between the two.

The scored results of this assignment could be considered by you and your student as either a process or product portfolio artifact reflecting the student's representative performance on daily lab exercises.

Synthesis Level: Students are able to assemble parts into a whole, formulate new hypotheses or plans of action, and construct solutions to unfamiliar problems.

During a unit on motion, your students could creatively design machines as a means of reinforcing previously learned concepts. Then you and each student could mutually consider entering the scored assessment of the student's design as a possible work sample in the portfolio.

Sample Daily Instructional Objective: In pairs, students will draw plans for the construction of a nonelectrical machine that will provide for the nonstop movement of a marble through its maze.

This creative assignment could possibly require more than one class period for its completion. Then, following assessment of the project, you and the two students could decide to enter the scored assessment of their plans as either a process or a product artifact in their portfolios.

Evaluation Level: Students are able to judge a phenomenon on the basis of predetermined criteria or internal consistency.

Currently, numerous science-related controversies rage throughout the nation. The position that one takes in these controversies often involves a value judgment. It could be interesting and revealing to ask your students to research some of these issues for the purpose of making rationale decisions. However, when assessing their decisions, remember that your assessment should be based on the rationale underlying the decisions, not on whether you agree with the decision itself. With this state of mind, you and your student may wish to consider his assessment as a portfolio work sample.

Sample Daily Instructional Objective: After a class discussion on the merits of traditional lab dissection and virtual dissections, students will determine which method they favor and give three written reasons for their choice.

Having assessed students on the basis of the underlying rationales of their positions, regardless of whether those positions coincide with yours, you and each student can consider the assessed paper as a possible portfolio artifact as a growth or product entry.

Social Studies

Knowledge Level: Students are able to recognize and recall previously learned information; no comprehension or understanding of the information is implied.

You and your students will want to select from among activities within this level as a means of establishing starting points for displaying their progression through the cognitive hierarchy of this curriculum. You and your student could examine the student's performance on a map-labeling exercise as an example of a Knowledge-level portfolio artifact.

Sample Daily Instructional Objective: On a blank map, students will correctly label the fifty states and their respective capitals, with no more than ten spelling errors.

If agreed upon as a portfolio entry, the scored rubric of the student's performance should be entered either as a process or a product sample, depending on the quality of the performance.

Comprehension Level: Students are able to understand or summarize information, translate information from one form or level to another, and comprehend data trends.

Translating information from one form to another is a Comprehension-level performance, easily demonstrated by your students by displaying data in different media, as in the following example.

Sample Daily Instructional Objective: Presented with a chart showing the Louisiana rice production for the past five years, students will display the same information on a line graph.

You and your student may decide to select the line graph as a representative Comprehension-level portfolio artifact, which can serve as a process or as a product entry, depending on the quality of the student's performance.

Application Level: Students are able to take information that has previously been acquired and comprehended and use it in concrete situations.

Being able to construct maps is an Application-level activity, as shown in the following example. Such a project could be jointly considered by you and your student as a representative portfolio entry.

Sample Daily Instructional Objective: Given the distance, to the nearest foot, between two points on the school grounds, students will each construct a map, with a legend, showing the distance between the two points, with a margin of error not exceeding five feet.

This assignment could be considered by you and each student for an Application-level portfolio entry.

Analysis Level: Students are able to break down a unified whole into its basic parts and understand the relationship among these parts, determine cause–effect relationships, understand analogies and metaphors, and classify phenomena.

Let's say you want your students to understand that there are both commonalities and unique differences among the religions of the world, as in the following example:

Sample Daily Instructional Objective: Following separate readings on Hinduism and Buddhism, students will list at least three similarities and three differences between the two religions.

Analysis-level in that it necessitates the comparison of two sets of characteristics, this objective serves as an impetus for students to expand their understanding of world religions, and the paper can serve as either a representative process- or product-oriented portfolio artifact.

Synthesis Level: Students are able to assemble parts into a whole, formulate new hypotheses or plans of action, and construct solutions to unfamiliar problems.

As part of a cartography unit, you could give your students opportunities for creative applications of content material that they have acquired and comprehended. Then the two of you may examine the written assessment of each student's creative performance for a possible portfolio work sample.

Sample Daily Instructional Objective: When presented with a U.S. map and the scenario that they are travel agents, as an extended in-class assignment, students will respond to a client's request for a "scenic but somewhat direct route from Houston to Philadelphia," by creating such a route on the map and then providing a one- to two-page explanation for the route they have drawn.

We suggest you assess each student's performance according to a very detailed rubric. Then, the two of you could consider the scored rubric as a possible entry in the portfolio, as either a growth or product work sample, depending on the quality of the performance and where the assignment falls in the semester's sequence. You could also consider including the map.

Evaluation Level: Students are able to judge a phenomenon on the basis of predetermined criteria or internal consistency.

A challenging assignment at this level would be to ask your students to evaluate strengthening or relaxing current emission controls. Then you and each student could discuss whether to enter the scored paper as an artifact in the portfolio.

Sample Daily Instructional Objective: After reading one article supporting strengthening emission controls and another supporting relaxing them, students will decide which position they favor and give three written reasons for their value judgment.

The objective calls for a value judgment that will probably be based on each student's personal criteria. Hence, it is important to assess the student's rationale rather than the position itself. Then, you and each student can consider the scored assessment for entry into the portfolio, either as a process or as a product artifact.

English–Language Arts

Knowledge Level: Students recognize and recall previously learned information; no comprehension or understanding of the information is implied.

Activities within this level establish a starting point for displaying students' progression through the cognitive hierarchy of the curriculum. The ability to associate punctuation symbols with their respective usages is an important Knowledge-level performance. One or two scored daily quizzes could be excellent representative samples of a student's learning the punctuation marks and their usages.

Sample Daily Instructional Objective: On a seven-item matching exercise, students will match at least five of seven punctuation marks with their respective usages.

If mutually accepted as representative of the student's Knowledge-level performance, a quiz like this could be entered as either a process-or as a product-oriented artifact, depending on the degree of the student's performance as measured by the standards of the objective.

Comprehension Level: Students are able to understand or summarize information, translate information from one form or level to another, and comprehend data trends.

With objectives like the following example, your students can demonstrate their comprehension of synonyms.

Sample Daily Instructional Objective: Presented with ten vocabulary words, students will write two synonyms for each.

You and your student could enter the scored paper in the portfolio as evidence of the ability to expand vocabulary through understanding that even complex vocabulary words have synonyms. Once again, whether the scored paper is to be a process or product artifact is a decision made jointly by you and your student.

Application Level: Students are able to take information that has previously been acquired and comprehended and use it in concrete situations.

The ability to write sentences in their various forms is an Application-level skill that spans the content areas, and documentation of this skill is a possible portfolio entry.

Sample Daily Instructional Objective: As a written assignment, with no more than a total of two mechanical or grammatical errors, students will each write a simple, complex, and compound sentence for each of the following types of sentences: declarative, interrogative, and imperative.

The corrected work can be entered into a student's portfolio as either a growth or a product work sample, depending on its quality.

Analysis Level: Students are able to break down a unified whole into its basic parts and understand the relationship among these parts, determine cause–effect relationships, and understand analogies and metaphors.

To enhance your students' understanding and enjoyment of literature, you can present opportunities for them to locate and analyze the structural features of their assigned readings. Then you and your students could consider entering the scored results of these interpretations as possible portfolio artifacts.

Sample Daily Instructional Objective: Upon completion of an assigned novel, students will explain, within three pages, the plot, two uses of symbolism, rising action, the climax, and falling action.

You should construct a clearly defined and multifaceted rubric for assessing this complex performance. You and your student could consider the scored paper for a possible growth or product work sample in the portfolio.

Synthesis Level: Students are able to assemble parts into a whole, formulate new hypotheses or plans of action, and construct solutions to unfamiliar problems.

After discussing the soliloquy as a drama component, especially while studying *Hamlet,* you could have your students write a soliloquy reflecting the process that they might undergo en route to an important personal decision. Then, upon return of the assessed paper, you and your student can consider it as a portfolio work sample.

Sample Daily Instructional Objective: As an out-of-class assignment, following readings and discussions of the soliloquy, students will write a one-and-a-half- to two-page soliloquy illustrating the process they could go through in making an important personal decision, including at least three steps in the procedure.

After receiving the assessed paper, a student could collaborate with you on deciding whether to enter the document as a growth or product work sample, depending on the timing and quality of the paper.

Evaluation Level: Students are able to judge a phenomenon on the basis of predetermined criteria or internal consistency.

With an objective like the following, you can give your students the opportunity to evaluate the treatment of sensitive issues found in their reading assignments.

Sample Daily Instructional Objective: After reading *Alive!* (Read, 1974), students will write a one-and-a-half- to two-page paper explaining whether the act of cannibalism was justified in this instance, providing three reasons for their moral position.

Despite your personal position on this issue, assess your students on the rationale underlying their positions. Then after examining the scored paper, you and your student can consider entering the document in the portfolio, as either a process or product artifact, depending on the timing and quality of the performance.

SUMMARY

Portfolio artifacts should be representative samples of both the curriculum and the student's work, because the inclusion of unrepresentative curriculum samples or atypically best examples of work only serve to distort and mislead. You and each of your students should select representative samples from each of the six levels of the cognitive hierarchy for inclusion in each portfolio to give you, your student, and the parents a broader and more accurate picture of the student's relative strengths and weaknesses. For example, you may learn that a student is having difficulty applying some of the concepts that were memorized because they were not comprehended.

Since learning should be a continual process, your students' portfolios should reflect growth. To show this process, the portfolio should contain work samples that show processes as well as products. If your students take part in the selection of their portfolio inclusions, they can see the progress of their learning, and they can assume ownership of it as well.

PROFESSIONAL DEVELOPMENT ACTIVITIES

In pairs according to subject area, review the definitions of the hierarchical levels. Now each of you write a couple of objectives for specific tasks, either paper-and-pencil or performance, for the different levels of the hierarchy. From these, together create a scenario of a student's degree of fulfillment of each of these objectives.

Now you are ready to role-play before the group. Alternate the roles of the teacher and student in a discussion of whether each record of the student's performance should be entered into the portfolio, and if so, whether it should be a process or a product work sample. Following each of the role-playing sessions, invite comments from the group.

WWW RESOURCES

http://www.miamisci.org/ph/lpdefine.html
This University of Miami Web site offers suggestions pertaining to the maintenance of portfolios that reflect student processes and products.

http://ncrel.org/sdrs/areas/issues/students/learning/lr2port.htm
This Web site of the North Central Regional Educational Lab offers suggestions regarding instruction to students pertaining to the content and placement of their portfolio entries.

Table 7.1 shows a few Web sites with information on portfolios and electronic portfolios.

Table 7.1 Portfolio and Electronic Portfolio Web Sites

Elementary Teaching Portfolio	http://primaryschool.suite101.com/article.cfm/ elementary_teaching_portfolio
Discovery Channel School	http://school.discovery.com/schrockguide/ assess.html
Technology Applications Center for Educator Development	http://www.tcet.unt.edu/START/assess/elecport.htm

Conclusion

In the course of this book, we have shown you how to deconstruct the standards of the major content areas by first modifying them and then converting them into unit and measurable daily instructional objectives with increasing specificity. You have seen how to write unit plan objectives and then break them into measurable daily instructional objectives using Bloom et al.'s (1956) cognitive hierarchy in each of the major content areas. In addition, you can now write a variety of test items that progressively ascend through the cognitive levels, and you are able to construct appropriate rubrics for the assessment of your students' written and performance-based activities. Then as a visible record of each of your students' performances at the different levels of the hierarchy, you can together categorize their respective artifacts into hierarchically organized portfolios.

The instructional and assessment hierarchy that is the heart of this book is a powerful vehicle, not simply another educational model for enhancing academic proficiency. It can provide your students with highly valued 21st-century skills, regardless of which vocational paths they select (e.g., Gewertz, 2008). These skills, identified by respected representatives of the business, education, and policymaking communities, are measurable higher-order thinking skills sought after in virtually every field of employment (for more information on these skills, see www.21stcenturyskills.org). Hence, through your students' progression through the cognitive domains, they will be able to make easy and successful transitions into their respective workplaces, where they can implement the higher-order thought processes that they acquired through your direction.

Further Readings

Alexander, P. A. (1992). Domain knowledge: Evaluating themes and emerging concerns. *Educational Psychologist, 27,* 33–51.

Anderson, R. C. (1972). How to construct achievement tests to assess comprehension. *Review of Educational Research, 42,* 145–170.

Arlin, M. (1984). Time, equality, and mastery learning. *Review of Educational Research, 54,* 65–86.

Arter, J. (1999). Teaching about performance assessment. *Educational Measurement: Issues and Practice, 18*(2), 30–44.

Arter, J., & McTighe, J. (2001). *Scoring rubrics in the classroom: Using performance criteria for assessing and improving student performance.* Thousand Oaks, CA: Corwin.

Arter, J. A., & Spandel, V. (1992). Using portfolios of student work in instruction and assessment. *Educational Measurement: Issues and Practice, 11*(1), 36–44.

Borich, G. D., & Tombari, M. L. (2004). *Educational assessment for the elementary and middle school classroom* (2nd ed.). Upper Saddle River, NJ: Pearson.

Brennan, R. L. (1998). Misconceptions at the intersection of measurement theory and practice. *Educational Measurement: Issues and Practices, 17*(1), 5–9.

Brennan, R., & Johnson, E. (1995). Generalizability of performance assessments. *Educational Measurement: Issues and Practice, 14*(4), 9–12.

Center for the Study of Testing, Evaluation, and Educational Policy. (1992, October). *The influence of testing on teaching math and science in grades 4–12.* Boston: Boston College.

Chatterji, M. (2003). *Designing and using tools for educational assessment.* Boston: Allyn & Bacon.

Davis, A., & Felknor, C. (1994). The demise of performance-based graduation in Littleton. *Educational Leadership, 51*(5), 64–65.

Dunbar, S. B., Koretz, D. M., & Hoover, H. D. (1991). Quality control in the development and use of performance assessments. *Applied Measurement in Education, 4*(4), 289–303.

Ebel, R. L. (1971). How to write true-false items. *Educational and Psychological Measurement, 31,* 417–426.

Ebel, R. L., & Frisbie, D. A. (1991). *Essentials of educational measurement* (5th ed.). Upper Saddle River, NJ: Prentice Hall.

Elliot, J., Ysseldyke, J., Thurlow, M., & Erickson, R. (1998). What about assessment and accountability:? Practical implications for educators. *Teaching Exceptional Children, 31*(1), 20–27.

Frary, R. B. (1988). NCME instructional module: Formula scoring of multiple-choice tests (Correction for guessing). *Educational Measurement: Issues and Practice, 7*(2), 33–38.

Gibb, G. S., & Dyches, T. T. (2000). *Guide to writing quality individualized education programs: What's best for students with disabilities?* Boston: Allyn & Bacon.

Gronlund, N. E. (2000). *How to write and use instructional objectives.* Upper Saddle River, NJ: Merrill/Prentice Hall.

Gronlund, N. E. (2003). *Assessment of student achievement.* Boston: Allyn & Bacon.

Guskey, T. R. (1997). *Implementing mastery learning* (2nd ed.). Belmont, CA: Wadsworth.

Haladyna, T. M., & Downing, S. M. (1989). A taxonomy of multiple-choice item-writing rules. *Applied Measurement in Education, 2,* 37–50.

Hasit, C., & DiOblida, N. (1996). Portfolio assessment in a college developmental reading class. *Journal of Developmental Education, 19*(3), 26–31.

Hebert, E. (1992). Portfolios invite reflection from students and staff. *Educational Leadership, 49*(8): 58–61.

Jenkins, J. R., & Deno, S. J. (1971). Assessing knowledge of concepts and principles. *Journal of Educational Measurement, 8*(1), 95–101.

Jongsma, K. S. (1989). Portfolio assessment. *The Reading Teacher, 43*(3), 264–265.

Joyce, B. G., & Wolking, W. D. (1988). Curriculum-based assessment: An alternative approach for screening young gifted children in rural areas. *Rural Special Education Quarterly, 8*(4), 9–14.

Kampfer, S. H., Horvath, L. S., Kleinert, H. L., & Kearns, J. F. (2001). Teachers' perceptions of one state's alternate assessment: Implications for practice and preparation. *Exceptional Children, 67*(3), 361–374.

Kleinert, H., Green, P., Hurte, M., Clayton, J., & Oetinger, C. (2002). Creating and using meaningful alternate assessments. *Teaching Exceptional Children, 34*(4), 40–47.

Kleinert, H. L., Haig, J., Kearns, J. F., & Kennedy, S. (2000). Alternate assessments: Lessons learned and roads to be taken. *Exceptional Children, 67*(1), 51–66.

Kubisyn, T., & Borich, G. (1996). *Educational Testing and Measurement: Classroom Application and Practice* (5th ed.). New York: HarperCollins.

Linn, R. L., & Burton, F. (1994). Performance-based assessment: Implications of task specificity. *Educational Measurement: Issues and Practice, 6*(2), 13–17.

Linn, R. L., & Gronlund, N. E. (2000). *Measurement and assessment in teaching* (8th ed.). Upper Saddle River, NJ: Merrill/Prentice Hall.

Macciomei, N. R. (1995). The effect of portfolio assessment on academic achievement and intrinsic motivation for students with specific learning disabilities. *Dissertation Abstracts International, 56,* 12A.

Madaus, G. F., & O'Dwyer, L. M. (1999). A short history of performance assessment: Lessons learned. *Phi Delta Kappan, 80,* 688–695.

Marby, L. (1999). Writing to the rubric: Lingering effects of traditional standardized testing on direct writing assessment. *Phi Delta Kappan, 80,* 673–679.

Meisels, S. J., Dorfman, A., & Steele, D. (1995). Equity and excellence in group administered and performance based assessments. In M. T. Nettles & A. L. Nettles (Eds.), *Equity and excellence in educational testing and assessment* (pp. 243–261). Boston: Kluwer.

Miller, D. M., & Linn, R. L. (2009). *Measurement and assessment in teaching.* Upper Saddle River, NJ: Pearson, Merrill, Prentice Hall.

Myford, C., & Mislevey, R. J. (1995). *Monitoring and improving a portfolio assessment system.* Princeton, NJ: Educational Testing Service.

Noddings, N. (1996). Teachers and subject matter knowledge. *Teacher Education Quarterly* (Fall Issue), 86–89.

Oosterhof, A. (2001). *Classroom applications of educational measurement* (3rd ed.). Upper Saddle River, NJ: Merrill/Prentice Hall.

Phillips, S. E. (1993). Legal issues in performance assessment. *West's Education Law Reporter, 79*(3), 709–738.

Popham, J. W. (2008). *Classroom assessment: What teachers need to know* (5th ed.). Boston: Pearson.

Rolheiser, C., Bowser, B., & Stevahn, L. (2000). *The portfolio organizer: Succeeding with portfolios in your classroom.* Alexandria, VA: Association for Supervision and Curriculum Development.

Shakespeare, William. (1965). *Hamlet.* New York: Dodd, Mead.

Shepard, L. A., Flexer, R. J., Hierbert, E. H., Marion, S. F., Mayfield, V., & Weston, T. J. (1996). Effects of introducing classroom performance assessments on student learning. *Educational Measurements: Issues and Practice, 15*(3), 7–18.

Slater, T. F., Samson, S. L., & Ryan, J. M. (1995, April). *A qualitative and quantitative comparison of the impact of portfolio assessment procedures versus traditional assessment in a college physics course.* Paper presented at the annual meeting of the National Association for Research in Science Teaching, San Francisco, CA.

Slavin, R. E. (1987). Mastery learning reconsidered. *Review of Educational Research, 57,* 157–213.

Stiggins, R. J. (2001). *Student-involved classroom assessment* (3rd ed.). Upper Saddle River, NJ: Merrill/Prentice Hall.

Swanson, D. B., Norman, G. R., & Linn, R. L. (1995). Performance-based assessment: Lessons from the health professions. *Educational Researcher, 24*(5), 5–11, 35.

Tanner, D. E. (2001). *Assessing academic achievement.* Boston: Allyn & Bacon.

Thorndike, R. M. (1997). *Measurement and evaluation in psychology and education* (6th ed.). Columbus, OH: Merrill.

Thorndike, R. M., Cunningham, G. K., Thorndike, R. L., & Hagen, E. P. (1991). *Measurement and evaluation in psychology and education* (5th ed.). New York: Macmillan.

Tombari, M., & Borich, G. (1999). *Authentic assessment in the classroom: applications and practice.* Upper Saddle River, NJ: Prentice-Hall/Merrill.

Wilson, V. L. (1991). Performance assessment, psychometric theory and cognitive learning theory: Ships crossing in the night. *Contemporary Education, 62*(4), 250–254.

Valencia, S. (1990). A portfolio approach to classroom reading assessment: The whys, whats, and hows. *The Reading Teacher, 43,* 338–340.

Walsh, W. B., & Betz, N. E. (2000). *Tests and assessment* (4th ed.). Upper Saddle River, NJ: Prentice Hall.

Wolf, J. S., & Stephens, T. M. (1989). Parent/teacher conferences: Finding common ground. *Educational Leadership,* 28–31.

Wolfe, E. W., & Miller, T. R. (1997). Barriers to the implementation of portfolio assessment in secondary education. *Applied Measurement in Education, 10,* 235–251.

Woolfolk, A. E. (1995). *Educational psychology* (6th ed.). Boston: Allyn & Bacon.

Worthen, B. R., White, K. R., Fan, X., & Sudweeks, R. R. (1999). *Measurement and assessment in schools* (2nd ed.). New York: Longman.

References

Arter, J., & McTighe, J. (2001). *Scoring rubrics in the classroom: Using performance criteria for assessing and improving student performance.* Thousand Oaks, CA: Corwin.

Bloom, B. S., Engelhart, M. D., Furst, E. J., Hill, W. H., & Krathwohl, D. R. (1956). *Taxonomy of educational objectives, Handbook 1: Cognitive domain.* New York: Longmans, Green.

Borich, G. D., & Tombari, M. L. (2004). *Educational assessment for the elementary and middle school classroom* (2nd ed.). Upper Saddle River, NJ: Pearson.

Gewertz, C. (2008, October 13). States press ahead on "21st century skills." *Education Week* [Electronic edition]. Retrieved December 1, 2008, from www.21stcenturyskills.org

Kubiszyn, T., & Borich, G. (2004). *Educational testing and measurement: Classroom application and practice* (7th ed.). New York: Wiley.

Linn, R. L., & Gronlund, N. E. (2000). *Measurement and assessment in teaching* (8th ed.). Upper Saddle River, NJ: Prentice Hall.

Linn, R. L., & Miller, M. D. (2005). *Measurement and assessment in teaching* (9th ed.). Upper Saddle River, NJ: Pearson, Merrill, & Prentice Hall.

National Council of Teachers of English and International Reading Association. (1996). *Standards for the English language arts.* Urbana, IL: Author.

National Council of Teachers of Mathematics. (2000). *Principles and standards for school mathematics.* Reston, VA: Author. Retrieved December 1, 2008, from www.nctm.org

National Council of Teachers of Social Studies. (1997). *National standards for social studies teachers.* Silver Spring, MD: Author. Retrieved December 1, 2008, from www.socialstudies.org

National Research Council. (1996). *National science education standards.* Washington, DC: National Academy Press. Retrieved December 1, 2008, from www.nas.edu/

Popham, J. W. (2005). *Classroom assessment: What teachers need to know* (5th ed.). Boston: Pearson.

Read, P. P. (1974). *Alive: The Story of the Andes Survivors.* Philadelphia: Lippincott.

Index

CORWIN

A SAGE Company

The Corwin logo—a raven striding across an open book—represents the union of courage and learning. Corwin is committed to improving education for all learners by publishing books and other professional development resources for those serving the field of PreK–12 education. By providing practical, hands-on materials, Corwin continues to carry out the promise of its motto: **"Helping Educators Do Their Work Better."**